FEMALE SUBJECTIVITIES
-
IN AFRICAN LITERATURE

Smith and Ce [ed.]

AFRICAN
Library of Critical Writing

FEMALE SUBJECTIVITIES - in African Literature
Smith and Ce (Ed.)

©African Library of Critical Writing
Print Edition
ISBN: 978-9-7837-0362-9

All rights reserved, which include the rights of reproduction, storage in a retrieval system, or transmission in any form by any means whether electronic or recording except as provided by International copyright law.

For information address:
Progeny (Press) International
Attn: African Books Network
9 Handel Str.
AI EBS Nigeria WA
Email: handelbooks@yandex.com

Marketing and Distribution in the US, UK,
Europe, N. America (Canada),
and Commonwealth countries by

African Books Collective Ltd.
PO Box 721
Oxford OX1 9EN
United Kingdom
Email: orders@africanbookscollective.com

Contents

Introduction   7

Chapter 1

Silencing the Abusers   9

Chapter 2

Subjectivity in the 'Eye' of Morrison   26

Chapter 3

Rotimi's Drama and the Gender Issue   50

Chapter 4

Rethinking the African Woman's Identity   70

Chapter 5

The Conflicts of Fall and Osammor   88

Chapter 6

The Women of Ousmane and Dlamini   101

Chapter 7

Female Subjectivity in Achebe's Novels   116

Chapter 8

Female Sexuality in Bessora's Novel   *138*

Chapter 9

Enekwe's Feminine Archetypes   *154*

Chapter 10

Women, Race and Liberation   *165*

Notes and Bibliography

Introduction

The New Female Subjectivities

AT some point in the so called advancement in human civilisation the patrilineal principle overthrew the pristine divine feminine taking precedence over the matrilineal in all civil, religious, political and cultural institutions. Socio-economic structures also became patterned to privilege the phallocentric order.

Through western civilization women have confronted what they perceive to be male domination of affairs in human society where it had seemed that facets of the society must conform to the male order before they are adjudged to be correct. The ensuing political strategy is to institute hierarchies that maintain and perpetuate male ascendancy and hegemony over the female. Under this asymmetrical terrain, the definition of individual subjectivity is executed essentially through the sieve of self and the other. A sexist and gender-specific monad in human existence has reduced individuality and refracted life and existence through gender politics and paradigms in the rigidity of maleness and femaleness without appreciating the complementarity of the two sexes.

In literature the ambiguous portraiture of female characters by some male writers and the phallic nature of men's writings have proved a matter of concern to female writers in Africa. For decades within African writing the issue of silencing was interrogated particularly as it addressed the muting and marginalisation of black women by male writers and the script of patriarchy which men follow.

In this series we continue the literary and dramatic tradition of feminist concern for women's issues, and we review novels, plays and poetry which demonstrate a commitment to exploring the challenges facing modern women in changing times and excerpting the issues of gender, feminism, identity, race, history, national and international politics specifically as they affect women. Female Subjectivities collectively answers the need to question and adumbrate the possibilities of literary revisions, showing what it would mean to revise even the Feminist psychoanalyst in a discourse on the subjectivity of women of colour.

Smith and Ce

Chapter 1

Silencing the Abusers

D Shober

FOR decades the issue of silencing has been interrogated within African writing particularly as it addresses the muting and marginalization of black women by male African writers and the script of patriarchy which they follow.

Chinua Achebe, heralded as the father of African literature, and renowned for his historical African novels as well as his textual and discursive criticisms of colonialism, was earlier taken to task by female critics such as Rosa Ure Mezu and Andrea Powell for his de-centralization of women as portrayed as portrayed within the African tribal community. Powell argues that Achebe's "historical novels consistently side-line the place of the postcolonial woman in order to focus on postcolonial manhood" (167). Achebe explores the hierarchy of gendered positions and the potency of African masculinity through Okonkwo the male protagonist of *Things Fall Apart* who affirms that "[no] matter how prosperous a man [is], if he [is] unable to rule his women and his children (and especially his woman) he [is] not really a man" (53). In many instances this control is exerted by physical violence resulting in his three wives living "in perpetual fear of his fiery temper" (13). Nor are the women in his two historical texts *Things Fall Apart* or *Arrow of God* ever able to find to relief or release from the aggressive subjugation under which they live. Yet in his fifth novel *Anthills of the Savannah*, Achebe does create a transformed female character. Beatrice is an empowered individual whose voice is that of prophetess and her role likened to a goddess (105). As Emezue underscores: "Of all the characters in the novel she understands at the end the importance of living a purposeful life" (250) and "recognizes the real meaning of human existence" (251), her voice radiates strength and vision to her ravaged community. But not all male African writers create such substantial, autonomous female characters.

Christine Obbo writes that "the need to control women has always been an important part of male success in African societies" (4), and literature, ever mimetic of reality has authentically captured this. Over the years, many black African women writers have been creatively correcting this notion of black African permissible aggressive dominance. Their narrative resistance to patriarchal subjugation and silencing has enabled them to craft female characters who voice their own autonomous, self-governing destiny.

Susan Arndt in her book *The Dynamics of African Feminism* notes that "African feminists hope to sensitize men to the discrimination which women experience due to the patriarchal structures of their societies as well as the behavior of individual men ... [and] count on men's fundamental ability ... to free themselves from discriminatory behavior " (73). But she warns that "men who disappoint this trust and are impervious to the emancipator endeavors of the women or even stand in their way are regarded as enemies against whom war must be declared" (73).

Ogundipe-Leslie articulated at the first Women In Nigeria conference that "men become enemies when they seek to retard, even block, these necessary historical changes for selfish interests in power, when they claim 'culture and heritage' as if human societies are not constructed by human beings, when they plead and laugh about the 'natural and enduring inferiority of women'" (82). Ama Ata Aidoo declares that "[u]nless a particular writer commits his or her energies, actively, to exposing the sexist tragedy of women's history; protesting the ongoing degradation of women; celebrating their physical and intellectual capabilities, and above all, unfolding a revolutionary vision of the role [of women],' he or she cannot be pronounced a feminist" (33).

The question may be asked how black African men have blocked or denied black women a significant place within, at least, literary representation. As at a least some of their novels reflect, seminal black African male writers have stereotyped at best or silenced at worst their female characters. Sindiwe Magona challenges this silencing and misrepresentation in her appeal to other black women writers:

"My beloved sisters, our men have not loved us enough, they have not honoured us enough; they have not respected us enough to make us equal partners. Thus, we have no voice. In the New Millennium, let us wait no more for their benevolence - it does not exist". ("Freedom" 21)

Almost in response such a manifesto, African American writer Audre Lorde recommends that women need to "transform silence into language and action" (40). Magona shares this view advising that a "revoicing" by black women writers is necessary "to fight our perceived insignificance – force our countries, our nations and the whole wide world, to take notice of us" ("Freedom" 22).

Although for decades it has been offered by such professionals as James P. Corner ("Stresses" 35) that black women have always been liberated (see also the research of Ladner, Stratton, and Lamon), others, such as the African male academic at the 2011 English Academy conference where this paper was delivered, sniped that black women need to stop talking about silencing and do something about it. And black women writers have been doing just that in a powerful and almost predatory way. As Weiss avers, women are no longer simply reacting or writing back, rather they are "taking action" ("Shades" 14), and although she may have intimated this in a discursive sense, some black African women writers empower their female characters to fight back against their unfaithful spouses who have attempted to silence them through psychological or physical violence. This narrative strategy is reminiscent of the South African advertisement against rape televised in 2009 in which the women were ripping off the duck tape covering their mouths. It was a dramatic visual promoting not only the voicing of the assault, but aggressive action against it.

African-feminist literature, according to Arndt, has taken action in three different ways, classified as reformative, transformative and radical. Whereas the reformative literature offers that men and women potentially remain united in a stand against oppression and criticizes men as individuals not as part of the degenerate male pack (83), transformative literature, on the other hand, is more focused in its criticism and questions whether men in general have the capacity or interest to transform (84). Arndt explains that "Radical African-feminist texts argue that men (as a social group) inevitably and in principle discriminate against, oppress, and mistreat women" (85). These male characters are portrayed as "hopelessly sexist and usually deeply immoral" and are written out of the story through their premature death (85).

Four decades of black women writers have aggressively ripped off the silencing duck tape of literary representation. Bessie Head's "Collector of Treasures", Mariama Ba's *So Long a Letter*, Yvonne Vera's *Under the Tongue*, Neshani Andreas' *The Purple Violet of Ashaantu*, and Sindiwe Magona's *Beauty's Gift* have inverted the paradigm of female silencing drastically, and in the process, voiced their rage at the black partner's psychological cruelty or sexual violence. They hush the spouse in the most dramatic way possible - through death.

Head's "Collector of Treasures" (1977)

In Bessie Head's short story "The Collector of Treasures" the reader is presented with a dedicated and long suffering wife and mother Dikeledi, whose husband's abuse and subsequent abandonment forces her to raise their three young children alone. After years of blatant, dog-like infidelity, her husband decides to return home expecting a hearty meal and a healthy marriage bed. Dikeledi, having successfully negotiated her life and that of her children beyond the oppressive bestiality of her husband, determines to liberate herself of her tormentor and the instrument of his perverse manhood. The story opens with Dikeledi's traumatic journey to prison where she will serve a life sentence for murder. "So you have killed your husband, have you?' the wardress remarked, with a flicker of humour. "You'll be in good company. We have four other women here for the same crime. It's becoming the fashion these days" (*Collector* 88). Dikeledi, when asked by her new jailmate how she killed her husband, voices her act in its simplest terms: "I cut off all his special parts with a knife" (89). Kebonye responds, "I did it with a razor" stating "Our men do not think that we need tenderness and care. You know, my husband used to kick me between the legs when he wanted that" (89). Kebonye reasons that she was doing her community a service by murdering her school-teacher husband. Repeatedly she had been forced to endure countless humiliations of him impregnating young girls. Finally, when another set of parents came to her to complain, she resolutely replied, "You leave it to me. I have seen enough."

Head, the narrator, intervenes at this point and instructs the reader on the men of the world: "There were really only two kinds of men in the society. The one kind created such misery and chaos that he could be broadly damned as evil" (91). Head graphically compares him to a dog who is driven by his libido, and blames him for the "breakdown of family life" (91). Dikeledi's husband, Garesego, was such a man. When he commands her to silently acquiesce to his return, she knows what awaits her and her family. In his absence "[she] had filled her life with treasures of kindness and love she had gathered from others and it was all this that she wanted to protect from defilement from this evil man" (101). Thus Head, who had carefully described Dikeledi's hands as instruments of gentleness and creativity that nurtured her family and her community, empowers those same hands to excise from society the cancerous boil her husband had become. Head's and Dikeledi's silencing is forceful and conclusive.

Mariama Ba's *So Long a Letter* (1980)

Mariama Ba's *So Long a Letter* records the emotional torment of Ramatoulaye, a woman who after twenty-five years of marriage and twelve children is abandoned by her husband when he silently and secretly takes a second, much younger wife. Although theirs is a Muslim marriage where polygyny is permissible, his absolute and open rejection and desertion of his first wife and their children defies their religious tradition.

After an extravagant and clandestine courtship, Modou continues to lavish his beautiful, young wife with baubles, bangles and banknotes and provides a sumptuous home for both his new bride and new mother-in-law while emotionally and financially starving his first wife and their twelve children. Yet in Modou's pathetic struggle to keep up with his energetic and virile wife and her night clubbing friends, he is stricken with a heart attack and dies suddenly. Because Modou has "morally and materially" abandoned and humiliated his wife, Ba interjects with the power of the pen, stops his heart and ends his life. There is a cost for marital infidelity no matter how permissible within the polygamous culture. Ba prevents Modou from further acts of betrayal and then works from there to empower his discarded wife Ramatoulaye.

From the onset of the novel, Ba enables Ramatoulaye to voice her heartache. To her friend Assitou she pens her grief as if the written word provides a buffer and a bridge to express her pain.

"And to think that I loved this man passionately, to think that I gave him thirty years of my life, to think that twelve times over I carried his child,. The addition of a rival to my life was not enough for him. In loving someone else, he burned his past, both morally and materially. He dared to commit such an act of disavowal". (*So Long* 12)

Although Ramatoulaye silently bears the sword of her husband's betrayal, not confronting him or demanding his attention, explanation or financial restitution, after his death, she is speechless no more. When Tamsir, Modou's brother approaches her and demands: "When you have "come out" I shall marry you" (57), she responds vehemently:

"My voice has known thirty years of silence, thirty years of harassment. It bursts out, violent, sometimes sarcastic, sometimes contemptuous... You forget that I have a heart, a mind, that I am not an object to be passed from hand to hand." (58)

Although Tamsir commands her to stop, she refuses: "Purge yourself of your dreams of conquest. They have lasted forty days. I shall never be your wife" (58).

Ramatoulaye proceeds to decline a host of suitors, refusing to humiliate a first wife as she had been or subjugate herself martially or materially to another man. Her actions communicate her independence and self-determination. She is silent no more. She has become what she heralded of Assitou, her divorced friend's victorious liberation: "There you were an innocent victim of an unjust cause and the courageous pioneer of a new life" (34). Yet it is unmistakably clear that it is only after Ba silences Moudou that Ramatoulaye is given the strength and the voice to speak.

Yvonne Vera's *Under the Tongue* (1997)

Vera interrogates the horror of incest, a taboo subject within African culture. Young Zhizha, during her mother's enforced absence, endures the repeated rape by her father, events so traumatic that she is rendered mute. Kopf writes: "Right from the beginning, Zhizha's first person narrative is abundant with images that show her tongue as an immobile, frozen and alienated part of her body", but later the reader learns that this is not just a metaphorical representation of silence but an actual one (6). When her mother Runyararo learns of the rape she murders her husband, silencing him forever and permanently preventing further attacks. Weiss, in her article "Shades of Uttering," writes: "the unspeakable is made public in an unspoken performance, in an act of murder and her subsequent imprisonment. She remains silent as the act of rape is too horrible to speak of, and can only be answered by another taboo: a wife killing her husband" (22).

In multiple ways it is her mother that gives Zhizha the ability to vocalize:

Mother calls to me in a voice just like mine, she grows from inside of me [...]. I change into me, and I say a e i o u. I remember all my letters. I tell my mother and she repeats after me and I laugh then I repeat after mother who repeats after me and I after her ... I have turned into mother, and she laughs because she has become me. The letters flow from me to mother. My mother's voice is resonant and searching. She says we live with our voices rich with remembrance. We live with words. (81 – 82)

Vera empowers the two women to speak through their actions. Runyararo voices her contempt at her husband, a father who would dare violate the trust of his child by stealing her virginity; her daughter Zhizha by hiding words within. Both have given to one another and the reader the gift of speech to discourse such a tragedy, but only after the abuser's voice is permanently terminated.

Neshani Andreas' *Purple Violet of Oshaantu* (2001)

In Andreas' novel *The Purple Violet of Oshaantu* the female protagonist Kauna suffers physical violence and sexual betrayal from her husband and is afforded insufficient support from her village and best friend Ali. Kauna bemoans her repression and the feeble guidance offered by the village matriarch:

What I most dislike about her is that she does either little or nothing for the women and widows who are mistreated by their husbands and in-laws, despite her position. She believes that marriage should be one miserable, lifelong experience. Husband and wife should fight every day, he should abuse her and the children, he should go after other women, otherwise 'okwa tulwa mo'. It is the way of the world. She never has anything good to say about marriage. (*Purple* 4)

Yet one village woman does speak against the abuse and her bold vocalization garners notable respect and produces fruitful results. "Mukwankala is well known for fearlessly speaking her mind. As a result she is popular among women, especially young women, and in no time women had gathered around her like bees around an exotic flower" (147). Mukwankala's candor is well respected by the village women and, as seen in the case of Shange, she even de-tongues the men. After Shange severely beats Kauna, Mukwankala vigorously and publicly rebukes him, stunning Shange into silence and compliance. He never beats Kauna again. Nevertheless he audaciously consorts with a mistress, even building her a house -something he had taken years to complete for his shamed and maltreated wife Kauna.

Andreas, after painstakingly revealing the years of cruelty and neglect that Kauna suffers, brings Shange's life to an abrupt and early end. He has just returned from his mistress' house, and enters his own home where he mysteriously collapses and dies. Initially, Kauna is blamed for poisoning her traitorous husband, but she forcefully denies culpability, courageously voicing her innocence. However, when asked to select someone to praise her husband at his funeral, she refuses. She chooses silence as an instrument of communicating her rage and disgust at his betrayal and vicious abuse. The family and villagers are shocked, and even her best friend, who has long witnessed her suffering, urges her to speak; yet Kauna responds unequivocally: "I don't care" (50). Kauna's reply indicates her advancement to autonomy. After years of abuse from an unfaithful husband, and a village that failed to intervene, she maintains her silence throughout the wake, refusing to mourn the deceased, saying:

I cannot pretend. I cannot lie to myself and to everybody else in this village. They all know how I was treated in my marriage. Why should I cry? For what? For my broken ribs? For my baby, the one he killed inside me while beating me? For cheating on me so publically? (49)

Kauna's independence stirs her best friend Ali to say with awe: "[T]here was something admirable in her behavior, some new strength that I recognized, and it was surprisingly heart-warming" (143).

In *The Purple Violet of Oshantuu*, Neshani Andreas not only silences the abusive spousal antagonist by abruptly killing him, she empowers her downtrodden female protagonist using the same device, slamming her lips closed and refusing speech as a form of voicing her resistance to his oppression.

Sindiwe Magona's *Beauty's Gift* (2008)

In this novel, Sindiwe Magona centralizes "the sociological and psychological aspect of black womanhood in South Africa" through her analysis of the sexual subjugation and suffering of black African women, especially as it relates to the AIDS pandemic (Chiavetta 172). The story turns on the fulcrum of trust and how lack of male fidelity is the deadly scourge of African women. The novel's title takes its name from one of the characters who is fatally infected with the AIDS virus by her wayward husband. Initially Beauty is silenced by her overbearing husband, Hamilton, who chases her concerned friends from their bedroom just as she is about to divulge the nature and extent of her illness. Through flashbacks the reader witnesses Beauty's deterioration, from the swollen lips to the skeletal frame housing blind eyes, as her emaciated remains ooze with angry, painful sores. Yet Beauty's love for her friends supersedes her pain and shame and, with the passionate fires of an evangelist, she delivers a final deathbed warning to her best friend Amanda:

Don't die a stupid death, like I am doing! Live!" she says. "Live till every hair on your head turns grey. Earn your wrinkles and, damn you, enjoy them! Enjoy every wrinkle and every grey hair on your head. Tell yourself you have survived! Sur-vived!" Her voice drops. "Live!" she says. "Don't die … like this… (*Beauty's* 74)

This is the foundation of Magona's novel. Women die because of men's unfaithfulness. Traditional cultural polygamy or the hegemonic controls of patriarchy can no longer be acceptable in a society beset with a deadly sexually contracted virus, and African men's resistance to behavioral change is killing African women. Cordelia, one of Beauty's five firm friends, violently attacks the men at one of the AIDS funerals: "African mothers, faithfully married women, are killed by men who will not stop sleeping around!" (70).

The men feel the heat of Cordelia's accusation and one weakly retorts that she must hate African men, a shocking indictment against an African woman who should live, breathe and sleep by the light of the African male. With this statement, Cordelia lobs her final volley: "I hate my black brothers, you say? You're damn right I do!" ... Only a fool goes to bed with the enemy – an armed enemy, at that. What do you think the black man's penis is? I'll tell you what it is. It is a deadly weapon!" (71). Stunned at her accusation that their instrument of manhood and insatiable sensations could be deemed a weapon, the men abruptly leave for a shebeen (African township bar). That is their domain, their location of power, where conversation and behavior is ruled by their desire and level of intoxication. The women present in that environment would not challenge their hegemony or diminish their masculinity with ridiculous moral requirements or social responsibilities.

According to *Beauty's Gift*, rare is the African man who practices sexual responsibility. When the women deny their partners' conjugal rights until they obtain an

AIDS test, the male reaction is one of violence and rage. Cordelia's husband gives her a black eye and openly flaunts his infidelity. Edith's husband Luvo takes her by force, while Amanda's Zakes ignores her. Only Doris' fiancée Selby agrees to testing, but only because the bank requires a test for their house loan.

Magona's novel portrays husbands in various unpleasant forms: Hamilton sports a string of mistresses; Vuyo is openly adulterous; Luvo rapes his wife; Selby cheats on his fiancé; and Zakes, besides his two illegitimate children, is a drunken coward. In all these instances, husbands pretend monogamy while practicing polygamy. They expect their partners to remain faithful to them while they fornicate freely without repercussions. They expect to say "I love you" and all to be forgiven and forgotten. They believe a bauble of jewelry and crocodile tears will remove the stain of their infidelity. They represent the hard reality of the culturally endowed African man, as Yvette Abrahams warns: "black men are sexist and the violent emanations of that sexism could well succeed in destroying the Black community" (424).

Magona ends her novel with death. At the beginning of the novel, Beauty dies through the unfaithfulness of her promiscuous husband; at the end Zakes dies by his own pusillanimous hand. Drinking himself into oblivion in order to dull the shame of his extramarital disgrace, he drunkenly staggers into the path of a car and to his doom.

In various ways throughout the novel, men had attempted to silence women against voicing the flaws in their relationship, their unhappiness with men's serial polygamy. But women resisted in numerous ways. Beauty's body, through her physical degeneration, screamed of the marital abuse. Finally, just before her death, her voice was loosed to utter a warning to her female friends: "Don't die a stupid death -like me".

Before Zakes death it was Amanda that utilized the tool of de-tonguing her husband by refusing to allow him to speak to her about forgiveness and reconciliation. Although she could not silence her elders, Amanda nonetheless refuses to listen to their counsel about marital restoration. Similarly when the drunken Zakes is killed, she not only refuses to listen to their accusations that her stubbornness caused his death, she actually shouted them down, utilizing her voice and her limbs by walking out the door. Even at the Zakes' funeral, she refuses her traditional place on the family dais, choosing instead to sit with her five firm friends. Through her actions, she loudly voices her discontent: "She could not honour his memory – or the memory of what they had had, which he had betrayed" (*Beauty's* 166).

In a brilliant narrational move, Magona chooses to silence Zakes rather than allow him to voice flimsy excuses for his repeated child-bearing affairs. His hit and run pedestrian death further underscores Magona's recurring theme: sexual irresponsibility begets death. Thirteen years before writing Beauty's Gift, Magona voiced her desire to champion black women's autonomy:

Let's say a woman is wondering whether it is a good thing or not to try to change this or that in her marriage or in her relationship to a man, and she finds a book that I have written where I say: "If you were good enough for him to come to you, you are good enough for him to treat you well. If he doesn't treat you well, you should take yourself back! (qtd. in Solberg 91)

The five works discussed: Head's "Collector of Treasures," Ba's *So Long a Letter*, Vera's *Under the Tongue*, Andreas' *The Purple Violet of Oshanttu*, and Magona's *Beauty's Gift* each offer readers the radical form of silencing the African feminist may take in muting the psychologically and sexually exploitive African male. Having discovered that efforts to be heard appear to have fallen on deaf ears, African women writers are taking their pen and erasing the perpetrators of humiliation and violence altogether, thereby vigorously voicing their resistance by silencing their abusers once and for all.

Chapter 2

Subjectivity in the 'Eye' of Morrison

S Poorali

ALTHOUGH widespread studies and cultural surveys have been done by psychologists, psychoanalysts and cultural researchers to demonstrate the close relationships in the construction of gender and identity, little has been asked, using psychoanalysis, about the delicate, intertwining and deep connections between race and identity construction. The initial desire to write psychoanalytically on *The Bluest Eye* evolved from the need to question what it would mean to revise Feminist psychoanalysis in a discourse on the subjectivity of women of colour. Because the psychoanalysis process has been practised almost exclusively with white subjects, and racial difference only an intermittent and peripheral focus of attention, the question inevitably arises as to matters black female subjectivity in a white-dominant milieu. Through the history of psychoanalysis little has been asked about what might obtain if gendered subjectivity were considered in terms of assumptions about whiteness and blackness since people tend to distinguish one another by gender (Abel 226). In gendered subjectivity 'race' and 'blackness' seemed to have nothing to do with the civilized white human subject (225). Freud's and Lacan's male dominated theories of sexual development, which could equally apply to women, reeks with the charge that it was narrowly focused on the subjectivity of White Europeans (Abel 223). It is necessary to note from the onset that Lacan believes that race and sexuality are inseparable. It means that by displacing the absolute and displaying the difference between men and women, they recode race as gender. Lacan also used 'The other' and 'The same' between existing conflicts. But it is a glaring point that Lacan's 'L'Aute' or 'big Other' has no obvious relation to colour, or rather, the 'Other has no 'colour' in his view. As pointed out before, race plays a trivial role in Lacan's discourse, but his notions are nevertheless applicable in a study of black subjectivity. The process of construction of self, in the assumption of Lacan, is initiated in the Mirror stage and comes to fulfilment in the Symbolic order. In fact Lacan introduces 'Imaginary 'and 'Symbolic' to the concept of child identity. For Lacan, pre-Oedipal child lives in what he calls the imaginary (quoted in Bertons 161). This stage as he stresses predates language and 'the child can not yet speak, it is subject to impression and fantasies' (161). So in the mirror stage, the child comes into the 'image which that world gives to us', not a complete one, but fragmented, distorted image, which leads us to 'misrecognition' (161). For Lacan, we need the response and recognition of others and the Other to arrive at what we experience as our identity. This 'identity which we acquire from the Other is a form of fantasy and misrecognition. It is by interaction with others that our identity constructs' (161). So we become ourselves by way of others' perspectives and others' view of how we are. We are also become ourselves under 'the gaze of the other or Great other' (161). This Other may be embodied in one's father or mother or, maybe, is not a 'concrete individual', but everything it is 'stands for larger social order' (161). The main part which Lacan always emphasizes is that this 'identity not only is subject to constant change, it can also never be coherent' (162). This unstable identity, however, emerges as the ideal only with entering into language in the symbolic where the child learns to confirm its identity, for example, by answering to its name.

Subjectivity and Identity in *The Bluest Eye*.

The Bluest Eye depicts the tragic life of a young black girl, Pecola Breedlove, who wants nothing more than to be loved by her family and her schoolmates. She surmises that the reason she is despised and ridiculed is that she is black (even blacker than most people), therefore, ugly. Consequently, Pecola sublimates her desire to be loved into a desire to have blue eyes and blond hair; in other words, to basically look like Shirely Temple who Pecola thinks is adored by all. Pecola soon after entering young womanhood is raped and impregnated by her father, Cholly. Her mother, Pauline finds haven, hope, life and meaning as a servant to the white, blond blue-eyed, clean and rich family to which he dedicated her love and her respect for an orderly life that poverty not afford. Unable to endure the brutality toward her frail self-image, Pecola goes quietly insane and withdraws into a fantasy world in which she is the most beloved little girl because she ends up having the bluest eyes of all.

At this point, one can pose a few hypothetical questions as to how race plays a role in determining subjective psychological identity. Do theories from psychology and psychoanalysis provide valid assumptions for black identity construction or re-construction? How much of the theory of Lacan can stand in a psychoanalytical reading of Morrison's novel under study?

The Imaginary Other: The stage of mirroring others

As the process of construction of self as social identity is initiated at the Mirror stage and brought to fulfilment only with the resolution of the Oedipal crisis, Lacan introduces the Imaginary and Symbolic to the conception of child identity. For Lacan the pre-Odipal child 'lives in what he sees --*'The Imaginary'*. This stage, as he stresses, predates language and 'The child can yet speak, it is subject to impression and fantasies' (quoted in Bertons 161). So what he does experience here is a set of unified image of its body, a 'Gestalt or organized pattern' (161). In the mirror stage, which is a forbidden realm for real image, we come into an 'image' which that world gives to us; not a complete one, but fragmented, distorted image, which leads us to 'misrecognition' (161). According to Lacan, a normal subject must eventually move from the mirror phase (The Imaginary) to an acceptance of the function and power of the symbolic. So Lacan uses the term 'imaginary' to designate the other of the subject's experience that is dominated by identification and duality. The imaginary is thus best exemplified by the mirror stage. Considering the statement that

I is an other, this other is encountered as the symbolic order, the organization of signifiers that surround me. This I, that the subject might project in Lacan's term as ideal ego, goes out the object and identifies with it. In this condition ideal ego appears at that point at which he desires to gratify himself to himself, or the point from which the subject will see himself, as others see him, or the subject internalizes and introjects the object into himself. (Easthope 49)

Let's elaborate this imaginary self this way: 'In the prelinguistic mirror phase', according to Lacan, 'the child from within I state of being, starts to project a certain unity into the fragmented self-image in the mirror' (62-5). For Lacan, 'we need the response and recognition of others and of the other to arrive at what we experience as our identity' (161). This 'identity which we acquire from the other is a form of fantasy and misrecognition. So we become ourselves by way of others' perspectives and others' view of who we are; 'we also become ourselves under the gaze of Other or Great Other' (161). This perspective explains why Pecola, recognizing her lack, attempts to fill it by identifying with the image of the Other. Thus Pecola relates, through desire, to all identificatory Others. Claudia, on the other hand, tries to understand her 'lack', as by encountering Maureen Peel, she asks herself, 'Why was it important? And so what?' (Morrison 74). She manifests attitudes of jealousy and hatred toward the 'completed', 'unified' image of the Other and, ultimately, acknowledges her difference from the Other (74). The contrasting attitudes toward the other between Pecola and Claudia actually result from their different relationships with their mothers. According to Lacan, the mother is the first significant Other with whom the child is united in the pre-mirror stage. In the Imaginary, the child recognizes the absence of the mother, and then transfers its desire for union with its mother to the object around it. In Pecola's case desiring a presumptive unity with the m(other) is lost forever. Lacan believes the crucial stage at which the child gives up the mother as love object and attaches to father marks his exit from what he terms 'the imaginary' and entrance into 'the symbolic order', the time which

the child is less aware of any consistent distinctions between himself and others, has no language, has no sense of loss, and thus has no sense of desire. It is only through acquiring language and passing into the symbolic order that identity can be assumed and this process goes hand in hand with the creation of the unconscious through the repression of these experiences, such as sense of oneness with the mother, which form part of the imaginary. (quoted in Watkins 99)

Like other feminist psychoanalysts who have drawn on object-relations theory, Nancy Chodorow sees gender as produced item, and maintained through cultural arrangements, rather than anatomical ones. In spite of Freud who establishes gender identity around the fact of having or not having a penis, she places emphasis on the pre-Oedipal attachments between mother and daughter and through this conception introduces 'the primary identification' in which 'gender identity' is retained through continued connection to 'pre-Oedipal mother'. She believes girls do, however, 'retain a stronger core gender identity than boys' because of the mentioned reason, but their 'secondary identity' psychologically is produced 'through culture and social positions' (quoted in Waugh 47). She illustrates that 'the mother while treating her son as an autonomous individual from a relatively early age, tends to cultivate a symbiotic bond with her daughter since she seeks unconsciously to re-create the intimate bonds she enjoyed with her own mother'(Palmer 31). According to Chodorow's notion, gender is produced through the earliest construction of a sense of self in identification, so the pre-Oedipal and Oedipal periods and the different ways in which boys and girls experience them, are crucial in reproducing the status of woman as the primary nurtures, because girls are parented by someone of the same gender or sameness. It is through this institution, rather than through 'anatomical difference that ability to the mother will be reproduced in the little girls' (Waugh 45). Throughout this phase, father is increasingly absent or is a peripheral figure that appears much more centrally in oedipal moment. Helen Moglen analyses this stage in *Redeeming History* and adds a new object to the pre-Oedipal mother-daughter relationship. She believes on the presence of 'the fetish object that is unveiled as fundamental and it is not the phallus as Lacan and Freud would have it, 'but the lost signifier that is the breast: the milk-filled breast of women' (Abel 207-208). Clinical findings also seem to support Palmer's, Chodorow's, and Moglen's assertion that daughters tend to remain in a much longer pre-Oedipal symbiotic relationship with the mother than do sons and refute

Freud's view that girls must renounce the mother in order to resolve their Oedipal complex.

Thus in accordance with stated subjects about mother-daughter relationships, Toni Morrison's Pecola continues her maintenance in pre-Oedipal moment, which results in lack of voice and nourishment to grow up. In other words, this occurs because of absence of the mother, who according to Lacan is a more elusive figure, 'one who enables the child's entry into a world of language in which she herself must always be silent' (209). Pecola's fixation in the pre-Oedipal imaginary is maintained, and her entry into and resolution of the oedipal complex prevented by her intense relationship with her mother. This is emphasized by Elizabeth Abel who says Morrison 'provides a version of psychoanalytic narrative that represents the mother as the irreducible matrix of the child's development, the unachievable object of a desire that cannot know but must forever seek its origin' (208). So the fact that Morrison does not designate Mrs. Breedlove as 'mother' implies the permanent existence of void, the absence of a m(other) in Pecola's psychic life. Indeed Pecola and Mrs. Breedlove have never had a normal mother-daughter relationship. Pauline spends all her energy on her employer's home and leaves her own home a cruel, black and ugly place. Throughout the novel, she never shows Pecola her maternal love. Instead she imposes a potential force and violence on Pecola. The main and manifest example is when Pecola enters inadvertently to a White home and frightens 'little pink and yellow girl' who spills blueberry pan on the floor in her white employer's kitchen. Mrs. Breedlove intensely reacts against her daughter, Pecola, and embraces the little white girl. As White girl gets the benefit of magically soothing language, 'Hush, don't worry none', Pecola shuffles away in abject humility (108-9). The theme the void of maternal self-sacrifice and its unhappy consequences is especially relevant to the episodes depicting Pecola's relation to her mother. A memorable episode in this novel which at some point explores the relations between mothers and daughters presents Pecola's and Pauline's strict relationship. In a heated argument involving her father and mother, as Morrison's narrator tells us, Pecola reacts by telling 'Don't, Mrs. Breedlove, Don't' (43). The narrator reveals us that Pecola like Sammy and Cholly, always called her mother Mrs. Breedlove. Superficially this mother contradicts the ideal mother in motherhood. This fact is also obvious in the selection of narratives in which every chapter opens with the explanation about Pauline which is juxtaposed with the explanation about White nice mother:

SEEMOTHERMOTHERISVERYNICEMO
THERWILLYOUPLAYWITHJANEMOTH
ERLAUGHSLAUGHMOTHERLAUGHLA

This extract, as Linden Peach explains in her book *Toni Morrison* 'is a way in which the white myths create an inner dislocation within Pauline that causes her to be less than nice to her own daughter. …in the white home in which she becomes a servant finds an order and beauty that causes to deny her own family and kids' (21). As a result, Pecola never adequately resolves her relationship with her mother, a situation which Juliet Mitchel states in *'Psychoanalysis and Feminism'* creates potential psychosis (288). Morrison's refusal to portray Mrs. Breedlove as a loving maternal figure, therefore, anticipates Pecola's crazed desire for love and satisfaction in the identificatory other. Her pathetic desire for satisfaction is resolved in her significant image of Imaginary identification -Shirley Temple, the icon of the ideal beauty. Demanding love and gratification, Pecola, sees the images of white as objects of imaginary identification. Pecola, the most delicate member of society; a child, the most vulnerable member; a female, and the other of the Other; a black, assumed her black subjectivity in subjectivity construction in relation to a white imago that reflects her to herself. 'She desires some milk in blue-and-white Shirely Tempel cup. Pecola was a long time with the milk, and gazed fondly at the silhouette of Shirely Tempel's dimpled face' (Morrison 19). And then: 'She took every opportunity to drink milk out of it just to handle and see sweet Shirely's face' (23).

    Pecola's reaction in psychoanalytic terms signifies her desire for Shirely Tempel, the racial other. Lacan believes that 'desire, in human being is the desire of the Other' (Lane 101). This Other, as Lacan asserts, is 'the locus in which is constituted, the speaking subject, which is linked to the symbolic orther' (101). For Lacan 'the object is the cause of desire, of that which is lacking.'(101). Identification thus occurs in terms of what is absent. By desire, Lacan means 'a striving for completion in that which is not wanted in any simple way. Thus where there is a lack, there is also a desire and a subject' (Lane 101). So Pecola metonymically shifts her desire for the mother, not to the image of the breast (milk-filled breast), but to the image of Shirely Tempel. By drinking milk out of the

Shirely Tempel cup, Pecola evokes in hallucinated form the feeling of contentment even in the absence of mother. Shirely Tempel, thus, assumes a maternal image to Pecola. This contentment is ultimately insufficient for Pecola who wants to be truly loved. Because 'need is governed by the interplay of satisfaction, and is the domain of real and demand yearns for the plenitude, which appears in the realm of the imaginary', thereafter 'desire is never brought to a close', because it fails to satisfy. Thus where there is a lack, there is also a desire and a subject' (Lane 101). Pecola's desire to be loved doesn't get satisfaction, so being loved by others was her ultimate desire. As, earlier in the novel, Morrison underscores Pecola's lack of love, she lets her ask a crucial question from Claudia about being loved: 'She asked a question that had never entered my mind. How do you do that? I mean, how do you get somebody to love you?' (32). The answer to her frequent question comes to her after she looks at herself in the mirror: 'It had occurred to Pecola some time ago that if her eyes, those eyes that held the pictures, and knew the sights if those eyes of hers were different, that is to say, beautiful, she herself would be different' (46).

She decides that a pair of blue eyes would make her beautiful and change even her parents' attitude toward her. Her insatiable desire for blue eyes is manifest in her overusing of milk from Shirely Temple cup. She has this rationalization that with blue eyes, she will be beautiful and her family will be transformed miraculously into a loving one:

If she looked different, beautiful, maybe Cholly would be different, and Mrs. Breedlove too. And maybe they'd say, 'Why, look at pretty-eyed Pecola. We must not do bad things in front of those pretty eyes. Pretty eyes, pretty blue eyes. Big blue pretty eyes. (47)

But her childish self-objectification fails, as the narrator says: 'She would see only that there was to see, the eyes of other people' (47). She only manages to see and objectify herself by the gaze of the look. She then finds the second object of identification, Mary Jane. Mary Jane, another indentificatory object for Pecola, accords with Lacan's assertion that 'desire is never for the same but always, is desire for something else' (Easthopoe 97). Pecola sacrifices much of her pride to buy candy for the blue eyes of the little girl depicted on the package because, she believes, 'To eat the candy is somehow to eat the eyes, eat Mary Jane, love Mary Jane, be Mary Jane' (50). Lacan repeatedly states that 'desire is the desire of the other'. This desire is an unconscious search for a lost object, lost not because it is in front of desire waiting to be refound, but because it is already behind desire and producing it in the first desire (97). Clearly, Pecola's desire to be Mary Jane is driven by desire to be the other. The same desire which equals to Lacan's desire, which is a metonymy of the 'want-to-be', the same unspecific but 'deep-self longing' (97). Recognizing that desire is without end and one can never get satisfaction which helps to keep him at a distance from himself. Pecola enacts an illusion of fusing with the other and thereby achieving an impossible plenitude-jouissance. The experience of Jouissance is usually sexual and orgasmic. Jouissance is a word which is translated into an 'orgasm' but in French it has stronger meaning altogether since it includes the idea of possessing something (Lane 102). In precise sense, the term here is 'proof of the other's existence', in Lacan's view 'the jouissance is of the other' (Lane 167). Therefore one can conclude that without the real jouissance, 'the other remains ultimately a fiction, a purely symbolic object of strategic reasoning exemplified in the rational choice theory' (168). Since the narrator tells, 'three pennies had bought her nine lovely orgasms with Mary Jane. Lovely Mary Jane, for whom a candy is named' (50). This desire I mean eating something like candy and getting pleasure of it has another meaning for her, if one accept Freud's view which, as Waugh states, 'can turn into an expression of tenderness as easily as into a wish for someone. ... like a derivative of the first, oral phase of organization of the libido, in which the object which we long for and desire, is assimilated by eating' (58).

It can thus be surmised that Pecola finds herself driven by a desire to eat Mary Jane candy and experience an illusory sense of Jouissance. Also Barbara Rigney has already indicated her objective elaboration on Morrison's novels that 'in Morrison's texts, food like everything else in her world is metaphoric, diffusely erotic, expressive of jouissance' (Mackay 88). Pecola feverishly desires this identification with Mary Jane, because according in identification of love: 'love is something, giving what you don't have' (Easthope 66). For Lacan, 'love involves a series of fantasy identification in which the object is taken up into the self' (67). 'First, the other as a whole is misrecognized and appointed as a single point. This is further misrecognized as the eyes of the beloved. These are treated like a mirror in the Mirror stage' (87). So the love to Mary Jane, here, based on Lacan's view, treats like a mirror in the Mirror stage, and reflects the lover in a more perfect form. The eyes of Mary Jane, which Pecola wished for, are imagined 'not as a passive mirror but as a person with an adoring gaze wholly occupied in looking at the viewer; in this look the lover is seen not as they are but as they want to imagine themselves to be. The perfect lover, the perfect self' (67-68).

A further step in Pecola's fall into the Imaginary realm occurs in her inability to differentiate herself from the other. For example, Pecola in the picture show, 'Imitation of Life', when she introduces herself to Maureen Peal, learns that the name of a young female character in the show is also 'Pecola', who is 'Pretty'. Although we do not know Pecola's conscious reaction toward this other in the Picture Show but one finds that Pecola implicitly identifies with the girl. Note that when Maureen Peal told about the girl on the show 'where this mulatto girl hates her mother because she is black and ugly' (67), Pecola responds with an 'Oh'. Claudia describes Pecola's voice as 'no more than a sigh' (67). Pecola in the Picture Show might be seen as her alter-ego. Or one could argue further that Pecola is eventually not able to distinguish herself from the other after she has maintained such an obsessive relation to the previous identificatory others. So she is already caught in the identificatory web of the imaginary. Pecola cannot get the suitable self-image in the imaginary because of her inability to differentiate or distinguish herself from the others. By assigning these blue eyes to Lacan's conception of Mirror stage, one can understand that Pecola Breedlove is always looking into the mirror held up to her by the White society. This mirror inculcates into her that she is ugly, black and poor, and the only acceptable figure for this mirror is one with white skin and beautiful blue eyes. This image, as she assents, is 'the ideal image'. Here she is not exhibiting stunning self-love and narcissism, but self-hatred, and this is her main problem in identification. Her looking at the mirror and seeing herself ugly promotes a sign of despair, self-hatred and lack of self-respect in her. Thus in the mirror stage she fails to identify herself. In other words, in Mirror stage she internalizes the dominant ideology of ideal beauty. In Lacanian term, it is The Law of the White Father, or the deep difference between her and objectified image that obliterates those trifling self-assertiveness in her. Consequently entrance to the Symbolic order causes her mental, psychological and physical destruction.

Claudia's case is different. The relationship of the two little girls in community, and their different reactions to involvement in the imaginary, counterpoints to Claudia's maturity in this phase. She gets self-image from the Mirror stage. According to Lacan's theory in the Imaginary, when self is able to differentiate himself from the Other, he can get the self-image. Claudia gets self-image in the Imaginary, because she is able to differentiate herself from the other. The major factor to her success and privilege in this realm is her mother. In contrast with Pecola, Morrison establishes a strong mother-daughter bond between Claudia and her mother, Mrs. MacTeer. 'The harsh condition of life, marked by poverty and a bitter climate, shapes Mrs. MacTeer's sometimes rough and cruel treatment of her children, yet in spite of her 'painful rebuffs' and 'unjust punishment' of her children, Mrs. Mc Teer 'is capable of soft music, warm laughter and an abiding love' (67). Although the same class of Pecola's family, her family works hard to keep themselves indoors. Unlike Pecola's house, MacTeer's house resembles what bell hooks terms: 'home place', the site of self-discovery (68). Mrs. MacTeer's unselfish maternal love is the very opposite of the barenness and self-righteousness of Pauline.

The novel opens with the story of Claudia vomiting in her bed. Her sickness during the autumn is oxymoronically 'a productive and fructifying pain' (12). While Mrs. MacTeer scolds her sickness, she also remembers her mother's 'thick and dark' love in the medicine that helps her daughter to fight her health: 'Love thick and dark as Alga syrup, eased up into that cracked window. I could smell it, taste it, sweet, musty, with an edge of wintergreen in it base everywhere in that house' (12).

Claudia, unlike Pecola, experiences a moment of reunion with her mother. This moment is crucial during the development of Claudia's subjectivity, for it will enable her to distinguish the other from the mother. Rather than embrace the racial Other as Pecola does, Claudia consciously rejects it in language and behavior full of bitterness and hatred. She admits, 'younger than both Frieda and Pecola, I had not yet arrived at the turning point in unsullied hatred' (19). Claudia's hatred toward the other is born of a painful recognition that the other cannot replace the mother; therefore, Claudia in the domain of the Imaginary, converts her desire for the mother into a hatred toward the other. The turning point in development, as Marco Portales suggests, 'is the point when we mature, when we accept the reality of us and so learn to adjust to our physical and mental surrounding with the world ground' (quoted in Feng 8). This juncture, perhaps, is when Claudia wants to enter the realm of the Symbolic. Until she moves into it, Claudia will never learn to accept the other. Claudia's hatred toward the other is intensified when the adults force her to love the doll baby, a mirror image that reflects her own unworthiness. Claudia escapes victimization by resistance to racial ideology and doesn't internalize it into herself. 'Her hatred to mass media icon Shirely Temple and desire to dismember the doll, manifests this resistance which takes a destructive channel' (Feng 70). Since Claudia cannot understand the universal allure of the white baby doll, she is possessed with an aggressive desire. As she says: 'I had only one desire to dismember it. To see what it was made to discover the darkness, to find the beauty, the desirability that has escaped me, but apparently only me' (20).

Yet Morrison is aware that the 'difference between Self and the Other is not only psychologically constituted but socially constructed' (Feng 71). As Claudia notes, 'Adults, old girls, shops, magazines, newspapers, window signs...all the world has agreed that a blue eyed, yellow-haired, pink-skinned doll was that every girl treasured'(20). Nevertheless, Claudia refuses to accept the value that resides in the baby doll until she understands how it is produced. Although no one tells her the origin of the belief system, Claudia generally realizes it as she journeys through mirror stage. As elaborated, these two girls' race and class are more important than their gender.

On a literal level Claudia's obsessive hatred for the white and her attempt to dismantle the doll, the symbol of whiteness, is motivated by envy of their social and economic privileges.

In spite of Pecola, Claudia is still in love with her self-image and feels comfort with her skin, as the narrator informs us, when she encounters Maureen Peal, 'colored' embodiment of the white doll, she is just curious about her skin which makes Maureen beautiful. She says: 'All the time we know that Maureen Peal was the energy and not worthy of such hatred. The thing to fear was the thing that made her beautiful, and not us' (74). Metaphorically, Morrison implies that the 'thing' is the phallus, The-Name-Of-The-Father, the ruling other, the same symbol which represents in patriarchal society, As observed of Lacan's notion of Symbolic world of differences, 'the phallus' is the privileged signifier which helps all signifiers achieve a unity with their signified (Easthopoe 102). In the symbolic domain', 'phallus is here king'(101). Claudia is educated by this sense of racial 'lack' through a mirror stage, the racial inferiority in unconditional admiration of white beauty, and so reaches the turning point in the development of her psyche. In order to survive as a normal subject, she learns to differentiate herself from the other, and accepts the social construction of the difference. As an adult Claudia records the account for the subjectivity:

Thus the conversation from pristine sadism to fabricated hatred, to fraudulent love. It was a small step to Shireley Tempel. I learned much later to worship her, just as I learned to delight in cleanliness, knowing, ever as I learned, that the change was adjustment without improvement. (23)

Claudia's small step to Shirely Tempel indicates her small step toward the realm of the Symbolic. For her psychic evolution to occur, Claudia knows that she must ultimately move into the register of the symbolic.

The Symbolic Other

One thing that forces Pecola and Claudia to enter the Symbolic order is the appearance of their fathers. Yet both of them fail to take up their symbolic function. Instead, a third agency represents the symbolic father to them. As Elizabeth Grosz elaborates, the dual imaginary relation needs to be symbolically regulated or mediated: 'This occurs with the help of a term outside third dual structure, a third position beyond the mother-child dyad. This third term is the father, not the real, but the imaginary father who takes on the symbolic function of law' (47). In Pecola's case, Cholly Breedlove, her father, fails to take up the symbolic function, because he is deprived of phallic power by White culture, the ruling Other in youth, and thus psychologically castrated. Since Cholly cannot remain in his proper place as the paternal agent to Pecola, he ironically violates his proper role and becomes merely a brutal, imaginary Other whom Pecola undoubtedly will reject. Pin-Chia Feng tells in his essay on Morrison's novel, 'The Gaze Of The Bluest Eye' that 'Without positive paternal role models and sufficient contact with the healthy influence of his agrarian community, Cholly is ill prepared for his paternal role, his migration and emotional tumult with Pauline contribute to Cholly's inability to keep his family indoors' (62-63).

Pecola's father literally and metaphorically is absent from her childhood. With his rather ineffectual role as a parent, he is never a sufficient authority figure to wrench Pecola through Oedipal stage. Since Cholly cannot take up the symbolic function in Pecola's post-mirror subjectivity, Soaphead Church appears as a representation of the symbolic father, performing the law of the father.

Soaphead Church is the character who seems a function, appearing only at the end of the novel. Although the apparent role of Soaphead Church is that of 'psychic reader', his actual role is like that of symbolic father. When Soaphead Church faces Pecola's request for the blue eyes, he senses his own powerlessness: 'For the first time he honestly wished he could work miracles. Never before had he really wanted the true and holy power' (174). His powerlessness in Lacanian terms suggests his lack of the phallic power. This fact contradicts Lacan's 'having and lacking' the phallus which is accentuated by Jean Walton and Judith Butler who precisely emphasize 'women or feminine position to be the phallus', to signify their 'lack and absence' of something which is 'dialectical' for the 'confirmation of their identity' (Butler 230). In fact, despite Church's masculine identity, he is the dispossessed phallic. So with knowledge of this lack, with anger and frustration, Soaphead Church decides to play the role of God, the ultimate Father. In his letter to God, he attempts to justify his 'giving' blue eyes to Pecola. He writes: 'I gave her those blue eyes she wanted. Not for pleasure, and not for money. I did what you did not, couldn't, would not do: I look at the ugly little black girl, and I loved her. I played you' (182).

Consequently, Soaphead Church assumes the Name-of-the-Father and gains the power of signification. He validates Pecola's wish for blue eyes, offering her an illusion of totality. Unfortunately, as a falsified father, Soaphead Church registers Pecola in the domain of the Imaginary rather than the Symbolic. As a psychic subject, Pecola ultimately remains in the Imaginary. She keeps looking at her 'blue' eyes in the mirror, and worries that her eyes are not 'the bluest'. Pecola, as Claudia describes, looks like 'a winged but grounded bird, intent on the blue void it could not reach' (204). In schizophrenic state, the final scene demonstrates complete breakdown; she is unable to distinguish reality and fantasy:

The schizophrenic, indeed, is one who, unable to organize, has no stable sense of identity, times or memory and experiences isolated, disconnected, discontinuous material signifiers which fail to link up into a coherent sequence. There is no persistence of 'I' and 'Me' overtime, only an undifferentiated vision of the world in the present. (Waugh 31)

Indeed, the void in Pecola's psychic life can never be fulfilled in the domain of the symbolic. So, what Pecola can do, is to take the imaginary for the real. Pecola's madness shows both how she has experienced to be a 'normal feminine' woman in patriarchal society and also expresses the dominating authority of the ruling Other, the White culture. Pecola's attempt to deny authority of the ruling other devours her, and thus drives her into a wretched isolation and abandonment of self-worth through the other's neglect.

In Claudia's case, her father, Mr. MacTeer, also lacks power of signification, and is unable to register his daughter in the realm of the Symbolic. Unlike Cholly who only inflicts pain on the helpless, Claudia's father functions as his family's guardian. She portrays her father as a person who tries to keep his family warm. Besides her mother's warm hands, Mr. MacTeer battles to keep his family from harm. Although he acts as a protector of his family, 'Wolf killer turned hawk fighter', Mr. MacTeer has to spend most of his energy 'to keep one from the door and the other from under the windowsill' (61). Under such a threatening and harsh reality, Mr.MacTeer is, at best, a paternal agent in his quiet way, smiling when the family boarder admires his daughters as 'Greta Garb and Ginger Rogers' (61). Instead, it is the ruling Other who instills in Claudia the sense of lawfulness and willing submission to social rules. Claudia finally learns to accept the register of the symbolic.

The signifiers of that register constantly appear in aspects of what Lacan calls the gaze, along with the metonymic imagery associated with it such as the eye, the look, and the stare throughout the novel. As adult Claudia herself notes:

It was though some mysterious all-knowing master had given each one a cloak of ugliness to wear, and they had each accepted it without question. The master had said, 'you are ugly people'. They had looked about themselves and saw nothing to contradict statement saw, in fact, support for it learning at them from every billboard, every movie, every glance. (39)

Apparently, 'the master' is the ruling Other who is the locus of law, language, and the symbolic. Claudia recognizes that the phallus lies only in the ruling Other, and that she comes at last under its authority in order to survive as a normal subject. Thus, Claudia like the rest of the community, is subordinate to the ruling Other. Aware of her own submission to the law of the symbolic, Claudia says, 'we were not free, merely licensed: we were not compassionate, we are polite: not good, but well behaved' (205). Yet, Claudia does not accept her socially designated identity easily and makes a gesture of transgressing the law by telling Pecola's story. Stephanie Demetrakopolous points out in 'The Gaze of the Bluest Eye' that 'Claudia does do the sisterly act of avenging Pecola by telling what she can of the story' (quoted in Feng 71). In some sense, Morrison under the dominance of the ruling Other uses Claudia and Pecola to develop their subjectivity in relation to those dominant images of which Lacan so frequently talks: the mother, images associated with her, identificatory object, and the symbolic presents of the father. As a speaking subject, Claudia represents a 'normal' as opposed to the pathological subject, Pecola. It is significant that Lacan provides no words to represent women's relationship to the Symbolic order. They even couldn't achieve their identification with it through identification with the father, with the phallus, as boys, the male subjects, do. Pecola and Claudia couldn't achieve identification toward their fathers, because according to Lacan 'for women no such identification is possible, they remain always marginalized within and by language' (107). Susan Watkins tells about this issue in *'Poststructuralist Feminism'* thus:

Lacan makes women something which does not exist in the symbolic order, but which, through repression of desire for the (m)Other, founds the creation of that order in the first place. In other words, it is the rejection of the maternal which allows the masculine subject to assume his privileged place in patriarchy, and the refusal of the awareness of linguistic play which, however temporarily, allows of the creation of apparently fixed meaning. (99)

Thus Pecola remains silent through the end. The only telling 'tapestry are Claudia and the Creator Morrison', narrating the story as a 'counter-discourse to Pecola's story of silence victimization' (quoted in Feng 71). Both haunted in the Symbolic order, Claudia transgress the law by 'story telling (and she) presses on wisdom and consciously changes herself and her community' (72). As Adrienne Rich observes in *'On lies, Secrets, and Silence'*, 'for an oppressed woman of color, more than ever, her sanity and survival depend on speech' (32). In other words, Pecola's experiences, according to Patricia Collins, is not 'gender plus race plus class but as the product of cumulative oppressions in gender times race times class' (quoted in Bryson 35).

Chapter 3

Rotimi's Drama and the Gender Issue

O K Owoeye

ALTHOUGH Ola Rotimi's dramaturgy is known to adapt Classical tragedy in order to represent history and act as a commentary on issues of tragic import in African society, his plays have severally portrayed the notions of such matters as tradition and change, the metaphysical and the very controversial issue of destiny and predestination using "the historical perspective to explain the man-God interplay in matters of destiny" (Elegbeleye and Adeoti 258). Rotimi's achievement in the treatment of destiny is patented in *The gods are not to Blame*, an adaptation of Sophocle's *Oedipus Rex* and such other works as *Kurunmi* and *Ovoramwen Nogbasi*. It is not surprising that critical works on Rotimi's plays have focused more on the above subject matter than women and gender issues in the stories. However, a close look at the works would expose the gender imbalance and patriarchal nature of the African societies in which the plays are set. The little significance of women in the plays may be due to authorial choice to adjust history for his artistic and thematic intentions. Adapting authors do not owe history the loyalty to historical facts and details and this enables Rotimi, for instance, to alter the type of death that Kurunmi meets at the end of the play, *Kurunmi*. Ashaolu comments that "although this historical tragedy derives directly from the 19th-century Ijaye Ibadan warfare, it casts a suggestive glance at contemporary socio-political events not only in Nigeria but also elsewhere in Africa". (99)

Anita Kern talking specifically of the prose genre makes the observation that "female characters have figured more or less prominently in various novels or short stories according to the writers' purpose or to their particular levels of consciousness regarding women". (157) Indeed in all the three traditional genres of literature, authorial perception has always been a vital factor in female character depiction. It then becomes obvious that the absence of female participation in the political process in Rotimi's plays, for instance, is attributable to authorial intention especially since it is a trend in his three major historical tragedies. The playwright appears caught in a patriarchal hold that makes him overlook the significance of women in socio-political struggles and familial aspirations thereby prompting the question: what could have been the benefit of complimentary female involvement as the protagonists in all the plays daringly battle to safeguard their physical and ideological territories from colonial and territorial invasion?

II

The gender situation in Rotimi's tragedies recaptures the African patriarchal attitude for which theorists of Feminism such as Buchi Emecheta and Carol Boyce

Davies have carved a domesticated version of the feminist literary theory, tagged African feminism. African feminism is a contextual appropriation of the tenets of feminism to African female gender realities, challenges and values. Emecheta comments on the pragmatic nature of African Feminism and says "African Feminism is free of the shackles of Western romantic illusions and tends to be much more pragmatic" (554). Davies also summarises the concept of Feminism from an African perspective:

> Firstly it recognizes a common struggle with African Men for the removal of the yokes of foreign domination and European/American exploitation. It is not antagonistic to African men but it challenges them to be aware of certain silent aspects of women's subjugation which differ from the generalized oppression of all African peoples. (563)

One factor responsible for the evolution of African feminism and which will continue to affect any ideology on the depiction of the lives of African women is the disparity between the family, social and professional experiences of the African women, both at home and in diaspora, and those of her Western counterpart. Yet African feminism still agrees with Harold Smith's claim that "feminism as an ideology attempts to raise the status of women" (4). However, rather than "intellectualising monthly" (Obafemi 87) on ideological terms and contents, it is more productive, to agree with Emecheta, that "there should be more choices for women" (556) and that it is necessary "to discuss the needs of African women today …" (Ogundipe Leslie 550).

Just as African Feminism is an offshoot of Western Feminism, Womanism, Sexism among others have evolved to tackle the issues of female marginalization. Names, terms and tags are really not of much importance and, in this case, may become irrelevant unless the theory or concept takes a pragmatic approach to issues of women concern. This partially explains why some women opt for a more definitive and practical version of Feminism: Womanism. Womanism is concerned with the black woman who teams up with the man in a bid to fight a patriarchy that transcends gender boundaries yet tackling women problems in a way that makes it a kind of Feminism still.

Manifestations of Feminist allegations of inequality, discrimination and relegation of the female gender are seen in different aspects of human life but they are pronounced in literature where it has formed one of the theories of literacy criticism. According to Abrams, "a major interest of Feminist critics in English-speaking countries has been to reconstitute the way we deal with literature in order to do justice to female points of views, concerns and values" (95). The impression and picture of women given to the reading audience by writers of literature are of utmost concern to proponents and disciples of the various types of feminist movements. Various Feminist critics have tackled African authors for what they consider a misrepresentation or insensitive representation of women in their works. What has been projected by Feminist voices all over is the issue of relegation and not an emphasis on the benefits that could accrue to society by giving recognition to female involvement in crucial aspects of life. The gap left by the nonappearance of women in political deliberations and governance is hardly pointed out as women only shout foul and sometimes muster sentimental support for their course. Such gap in the male-dominated world of Rotimi's drama and the consequences, therefore, deserve a scholarly attention.

III

Rotimi's lead characters are often created with congenital weaknesses which could have been doused by the natural instincts and other virtues of women had the opportunity been given them to participate in the process of governance. The silence over the role of women in the battle against domination especially in *Kurunmi* and *Ovonranwen Nogbaisi* are both historical and artistic, engendered by the refusal to give, in the words of Ajayi,

Recognition to the silent behind-the-scene roles that women have always played in national, social, political, or economic struggles but which remain unsung and are routinely ignored in historical accounts and other documents, under the guise of general or topic-oriented accounts, the gender specific contributions of women are glossed over while male individuals are singled out for their 'manly deeds' (97)

Apart from the refusal to recognise the contributions of women in a revolution, some women's capacity is vitiated by the denial of the opportunity to perform. This is what obtains in the case of Princess Evbakhavbokun of *Ovonramwen Nogbaisi* whose pragmatic and sensitive approach to the political quandary ravaging the land of Benin at the beginning of the play is essentially feminine and result oriented. At a time when the king is threatened by external invasion and treachery within, the Ifa Priest from Ife is brought to foresee the general current of his regime. The divination turns out so unfavorable that even the diviner is wary of saying the whole truth. Only the Princess, the female present there, has the boldness to prod the truth.

IFA PRIEST: (with a shrug of the shoulders). It is well then. (Re-arranges the 'opele' beads in the original formation). Oba Alaiyeluwa, Lord of Benin ..... the shadows I see over your empire are heavy. Too heavy. Heavy... and dark.
UZAZAKPO: What does that mean?
IFA PRIEST: His reign is full of danger
EVBAKHAVBOKUN: Is it death?
IFA PRIEST: It is ... death
OVONRANWEN: (visibly shaken, rises and moves away a couple of paces) I shall be next victim of plotting then – my dead body following that of Uwangue Egiebo.
IFA PRIEST: Your Highness ... the death I see here is not the death of one man. Bodies of men . . . Fire ... and blood – bodies floating –
UZAZAKPO: An epidemic.
OVONRAMWEN: Civil war – the final curse of internal intrigues!
IFA PRIEST: That is my story: what I saw, I have told you. To say more is to lie (Rising).
EVBAKHAVBOKUN: What can we do to avoid this fire?
IFA PRIEST: Caution ... that is the word – caution. (15)

In this conversation we see Evbakhaubokun displaying a combination of bravery and reasoning when the men folk have already been held by fear and anxiety over the prediction. Her pointed question makes the Ifa Priest drop his diplomatic cover to solve his own riddle and declare that what he really sees is death. While Ovonramwen and Uzazapo react poignantly to the development, Evbakhavbokun still summons the courage to ask for a way out before the Ifa Priest leaves. The news of looming tragedy on the empire affects everyone yet it is the Princess who remembers that it is not customary to allow a messenger of the gods go away empty handed hence she approaches her father on the issue.

EVBAKHAVBOKUN: Father, what shall we give him? It is not right to send him away to Ife without a gift.(Ovoranmuwen is lost in thought)

UZAZAKPO: You go and find him anything you deem fit, woman. You are the Oba's eldest daughter – your choice of gift would be just as noble. Go on. (16)

Apparently Evbakhavbokun takes charge of the situation and arranges something worthwhile for the Priest to take back to Ife, likely without the knowledge of her grief-ridden father. With this display of diplomatic acumen, Evbakhavbokun promises to be a great ally with the men, ready to work and squash the rebellion growing in Benin and outside. In spite of this immense potential in Evhakhavbokun, this scene here is the only place where she has such opportunity to express herself and contribute to the affairs of state. The next time the Princess appears on stage is when she is married to Ologbosere without prior notice in the attempt by Ovonramwen to assure Ologbosere of the king's good intention and also secure Ologbosere's loyalty. Henceforth nothing is heard of the Princess who is expected thereafter to settle into womanhood, motherhood and home keeping and no one takes up her role in the king's court.

In effect, Evhakhavbokun's ability to handle political stress and pressure with composure is unnoticed and the absence of anyone to pick up this role leads to the king's inability to properly manage similar circumstances afterwards. Later when Ovonranmwen has the intricate choices of either pleasing the gods or the White man he only sings "the word is caution" unconvincingly to a set of chiefs who ignore his call and go ahead to kill a white man. This turns out to be the albatross round the king's neck for the rest of his reign. All through the scenes that follow till the final humiliation of Ovoranmwen, the absence of Princess Evabakhavbokun and her ability to discern what to do at the nick of time is only too conspicuous. The king's retinue of wives who form part of the cast are not given any chances either; they only sing and perform other supplementary roles that have no direct impact on the course of dramatic action in the play hence we can say that the world of the play is a male dominated one, accompanied by male oriented mistakes. This absence of female influence in *Ovonramwen Nogbaisi* and the attendant tragedy is similar to what obtains in *Kurunmi,* another gender polarised play by the same playwright.

The absence of any form of female voice/advice in Kurunmi's life aggravates his mistakes and his tragedy.

The act of delegating his five sons to go and "defend Iwawun or there die" (61) for instance evinces total absence of any form of motherly, wifely or sisterly influence which might have insisted on splitting the children instead of stationing the entire five of them on the same very hot spot in battle. The intransigence of the Field Marshal has either enhanced the silence of the women in his life or has driven them all to silence and irrelevance. Mosadiwin, Kurunmi's wife is only called upon when Kurunmi needs her to bring the soup with which he would send the incendiary message of contempt and disgust to the newly crowned Alafin Adelu and her only statement throughout the entire play is her clarifying question "Just the stew and ladle?"(25).

Thoroughly preoccupied with the contemplations of war and war strategies, the war hungry men of Ijaye give no room for female involvement that could have mitigated their aggressiveness. While they get incensed by matters of tradition and kingship succession, none is able to shift the gaze to the domestic side of life and attempt an evaluation of what a war of that magnitude may cost the citizenry. Kurunmi is a war strategist with laurels to his name but the circumstances surrounding the Ijaye war reveal that he is either ill-advised or lacks sound advice entirely. First he is a lone ranger in the cause, for other kings have accepted Adelu as the new Alafin. Considering the fact that the historical character transposed as Kurunmi in the play is described as "a bloodthirsty tyrant" who was "more dreaded in Ijaye than even the gods." (Johnson 283-284), it is understood that the women in his life and other denizens of the palace go into hiding leaving him without the kind of maternal protection that can be given only by women.

Kurunmi thus turns out to be the bloodiest of all Rotimi's historical tragedies. The aftermaths of the war last decades after it is fought and lost and, unfortunately, leave imprints on men, women and even children of Ijaye. Although the play does not contain the reactions of Mosadiwin to the death of her five sons, she is however present when Kurunmi poisons himself and insists that she should have him buried in the River Ose. Immediately he drinks the poison and leaves instructions for his burial, Kurunmi commands Abogunrin and Mosadiwin to "go now and ready yourselves" (94) for his unusual burial. The stage direction thereafter says "Abogunrin and Mosadwin exit" (94). This scene displays the insensitivity of the playwright to familial feelings especially since this portion is not culled directly from history but a fictive addition of the author to the legendary story of Kurunmi of Ijaye. The unrealistic manner of making a woman watch her husband take poison and exit calmly afterwards portrays that not only the Ijaye society of the 19th century but equally the playwright himself is too preoccupied with the exigencies of political issues to take cognizance of women's sensitivity. This becomes more probable just as in *Kurunmi,* a play sourced from history, as well as *The Gods Are Not To Blame,* carved out of ancient Greek *Oedipus Rex* by Sophocales.

The Gods Are Not To Blame has been studied variously as the tragedy of a prince fated to be a patricide and a regicide right from birth but less attention has been paid to how the tragic hero's human relations contribute to the accomplishment of the prophecy. The play contains a fairly larger number of women than *Ovonramuwen Nogbaisi* or *Kurunmi* though the balance tilts towards the male side. The women too are more conspicuous than in the two other plays. However, the customs and traditions within which the women are located ineluctably confine them to a form of silence and utmost submission even where their lives and happiness are concerned. Although it can be conceded that the oracle already predicts Odewale's patricidal and incestuous crimes, the culture of agnatic marriage which hands over a woman to her husband's successor the way other properties are transferred is a huge factor in facilitating the god's prediction.

It is discovered that all the characters involved in the prophecy make efforts to forestall its manifestation: Adetusa and Ojuola connive to murder the unfortunate baby rather than allow it grow and destroy their lives, Odewale himself flees Ijekun Yemoja in order to avert the evil prophecy looming over his head. While the unstoppable hands of fate are discernible in the eventual manifestation of the negative destiny, some other factors also contribute to the fulfillment which 'include the supernatural forces, the society, and the protagonist's personal weakness or tragic flaws (hubris)" (Dasylva, 19). Out of these three, Augusto Boal thinks that "he himself, by his own decision, moves towards his misfortune. It is intolerance that causes him to kill an old man, who happens to be his father, because the latter did not treat him with proper respect at a crossroads" (19).

If we follow the trend of Boal's argument and discountenance the gods, albeit temporarily, there are obvious human and societal forces in Odewale's tragedy.

First of the human inputs involved in the manifestation of this tragedy is Alaka's refusal to heed royal instruction and kill the child, followed by Odewale's disobedience to the oracle's injunction for him to "stay where you are" (60) when he goes to consult it in Ijekun. Odewale's inveterate temper is another major human flaw which enhances the fulfillment of the first part of the prophecy.

Perhaps the highest of the human factors contributing to Odewale's tragedy is the culture which turns over a man's wife, alongside with other properties, to his successor. This is an African leviratic marriage tradition employed usually in cases of childlessness. In Yorubaland the African widow is still given to the appropriate male in her late husband's family even when her first marriage is fruitful (Johnson 115). It is interesting that the custom is found in Classical Greece as well as among the Yoruba. The practice is more profound in royal settings where the next king automatically becomes the husband of the surviving wives of the dead king. This is the case with Odewale who traditionally assumes the position of husband to Ojuola as soon as he ascends the throne of Kutuje thus fulfilling the second part of the prediction.

Apart from being grossly insensitive to women as grief over the loss of a dear one is conflated with pains of an untoward marriage, this type of marriage has a way of conversely affecting even the man too, although gratified by the prospects of bagging another wife, a younger woman or secretly admired in-law unwittingly invite the angst of some other rivals in the household. Aderopo is one of such rivals and the tantrums that trail his relationship with Odewale are traceable to his hidden dislike for the fact that one who is only two years older than he and consequently his age group, is now husband to his mother. The following altercation between him and Odewale displays his discomfort at the marriage combination:

ODEWALE: Just because I am an Ijekun man, and do not belong to your tribe, the sight of me as your king gnaws at your liver, and rips your heart asunder. So you go round me, bribe that blind but to come and point his finger at me as the cursed killer of your father. Tell me now, is that not the act of crawling, cunning tortoise?

ADEROPO: Your highness, I have been taking all these insults from you because you married my mother and custom demands that I...

ODEWALE: Ah, I thank you. Bedsharer. I forget that one. The blind bat called me bedsharer too. Tell me, what is the crime I have committed by marrying your mother and raising children by her? (34)

Aderopo is quick to redirect the discourse from the accusations of treachery and connivance to the issue of the king's marriage to his mother. Aderopo had earlier challenged the king to face him man to man rather than invite Ojuola, Aderopo's mother and now the king's wife to mediate between them. The king's ire equally betrays what might have been earlier misgivings on the marriage. Imbalanced as the marriage between Odewale the king and Ojuola may seem because of the age difference, the woman's attributes of submission, humility and self control could have been exploited to the king's advantage. Her calmness and patience contrast sharply with Odewale's irascibility and petulance. His verbal acknowledgement of her virtues when he goes to confess at the shrine -

ODEWALE: Gods! What a woman (*Kneels before the household shrine, arms raised*) Give me some of her patience, I pray you. Some ... some of her cool heart ... let her cool spirit enter my body, and cool the hot, hot, hotness in my blood – the hot blood of a gorilla! (*Cleansing himself in the sacred water*) Cool me, Ogun, cool me. (39)

does not seem to have any transforming effect on his character for almost immediately after it is rendered, he goes ahead to show his knack for quick temper.

ODEWALE: Labata!
(enter Labata and Ojuola)
LABATA: Were you calling, my Lord?
ODEWALE: Have the chiefs not come yet?
LABATA: No, my Lord
ODEWALE: (angrily) Go and tell them I am waiting. (50)

Neither does he display any change in attitude toward his wife Ojuola who calmly and respectfully approaches him and asks:

OJUOLA: When will my lord come back home?
ODEWALE: Come back home? When you see me, you see me, woman. (51)

The tone of finality and emphasis employed in the word 'woman' is intended to remind Ojuola that she is a woman and should, therefore, not ask too many questions or attempt to control his movements. The various usages of 'woman' and 'wife' to address his wife reveals that Odewale is gender sensitive and would not do anything to appear a weakling. In the tragic discovery of Odewale's pedigree, the fatal blows directly affect the woman at the centre of the fulfilment -Ojuola. Whereas the females in *Ovonramwen Nogbaisi* and *The Gods Are Not To Blame* suffer indirectly from the tragedies through the death of either husbands or sons, Ojuola is at the centre of action in *The gods are not blame* and the tragedy is driven faster by society's perception of her as a woman. She is the one who gets disgraced at the end for marrying her own son yet she has no say in the decision on whom to marry. Her visibility throughout the play is thus because the tragedy is anchored on the role she is made to play by custom and tradition. After these three historico-monarchical tragedies, Rotimi makes a turn around and writes another play which is both a comedy and a departure from the male-centeredness of the previous three.

Our Husband Has Gone Mad Again appears to be an attempt at correcting the outmoded perception of women in his first three plays although in an environment that still betrays Rotimi's entanglement with patriarchy. The Nigerian dramatic scene had already witnessed the production of plays that valourised women by the time *Our Husband Has Gone Mad Again* was published in 1977. Femi Osofisan, for instance, writes to "highlight ... women's valour, as well as their suffering, and ... the unbelievable injustice of which they are victims" (8).

Osofisan's drama bears some resemblance to Rotimi's in that he also writes from history and myth but he creates eponymous plays such as *Tegonni: An African Antigone* and *Morountodun* where his heroines make positive contributions to society and cause revolution through heroic deeds.

Rotimi is not the only one to change his stance on the female figures in his plays, Wole Soyinka also in a latter play, *The Beatification of Area Boy* creates a female character, Miseyi, who teams up with the male ideologue, Sanda and they jointly stir a revolution. What we find in *Our Husband Has Gone Mad Again* may thus be part of the results of the clamour for better female presentation in drama texts by African Feminists.

Women in *Our Husband Has Gone Mad Again* are chauvinistically located in men's world but here they are seen striving to better their own lots and make their voices heard rather than the fatal submission of the women in Rotimi's earlier plays. The imbalance in gender relations in the play is engendered by Lejoka-Brown's parochial view of women in the family and society at large. The mode and purpose of acquiring his first two wives show that women are better reckoned within the confines of tradition or for some other pragmatic purposes. He marries Mama Rashidat because tradition requires it and Sikira because it will be of some calculated benefit to his political ambition.

The effect of these marriages on the entire family is that everyone is Machiavellian on most issues and this has retarding implications on the goals set both as individuals and as family. Lejoka-Brown confesses to Okonkwo that his marriage to Sikira is "...for emergency...that woman's case is only for necessity, anyway - temporary measure. We need women's votes, man, if we must win the next election" (10). Thus Sikira packs her belongings and leaves Lekoja-Brown's house when she discovers that she is only a means to an end for her husband, without considering whether her move would jeopardize his political ambitions. Even Mama Rashida is not committed to Lekoja-Brown's progress and responds swiftly to Sikira's teasing thus:

SIKIRA: Can you imagine? In three months' time Mama Rashida will make so much profit from Chicken eggs that the master will have enough money to borrow for his crazy politics.

MAMA RASHIDA (defiantly): Borrow my profits! To campaign politics? Allah forbid! (49-50)

The seeming subservience of the women at the beginning of the play is therefore only an outward show, a front put up to ward off critical and punitive offensive from their overbearing husband. Hence at the first exposure to the thought of freedom and equity, they all bolt. Whatever advantage Lekoja-Brown hopes to derive from them gets blown and it becomes obvious to him so he shifts position and later admits that men and women are created equal as he realises the women can no longer be held in perpetual bondage. He confesses to Okonkwo:

LEJOKA-BROWN: We have come to new world, brother. A woman's world. (71)

The play is a correction of the traditional view of the women in the three earlier plays of the playwright. Liza is portrayed as a woman of great skills and it takes her ingenuity to rectify the complex family situation created by Lekoja-Brown's ineptitude as a family man and rescue the two older women from atrophy. As Sikirat goes into politics and Mama Rashida ventures into business, the main thesis of the play thus seems to be Liza's idea that men and women are created equal. However, she has redirected Lejoka-Brown's lifestyle from that of "matrilineal polygamy to a Euro-Christian conjugal monogamy" (Dako 161). Lejoka-Brown at the beginning of the play is obviously a confused individual without deep convictions. After legally marrying Liza in the Congo, he returns to Nigeria and insists that the other women must "remain in the dignity and protection of this house of my fathers" (12). The contradiction immanent in his life is partially resolved by Liza's initiative. He is evidently delighted in her inventiveness from the way he swiftly reacts to Mama Rashida's request to relocate to the village and expand her chicken eggs business. Thus Rotimi shifts his stand and adjusts this play to "the status of women in the changing socio-cultural order" (Dako 158).

A holistic appraisal of polygamy in the play as distinct from the responses of individual wives to personal exploitation however is surely not positive and this may, if viewed separately, question the earlier claim that *Our Husband* is redemptive of Rotimi's male-dominated dramaturgy. Certainly Lejoka-Brown's cockeyed perception of the female gender is no better than either of Odewale or Kurunmi even in the twentieth century when the play is set, considering the way he sets out to maintain his patriarchal heritage and remain the lord of his household. What we here affirm is that the transformation he passes through until he settles down to tentative monogamy is an improvement on the older plays. Besides, the fact that the women strive to be heard at all, in contradiction to what obtains in the tragedies, is an improvement on Rotimi's work.

IV

Liza is a prototype African feminist after the order of Emecheta who obviously believes there should be more choices for women. There are certainly no choices for any of Evbhakavbokun, Mosadiwin or Ojuola who are compelled to chart the course mapped out for them by ageless tradition despite the auspiciousness of their characters. Ojuola, like any other woman, would definitely have preferred not to marry a man young enough to be her son if she had a choice. Liza's approach is to create choices for Sikira and Mama Rashidat through empowerment and orientation. She has her own choices too from the beginning to the end of the play; she could leave Lejoka-Brown or stay married to him if she so desired. A comparative study of the two groups of women would reveal that family, society, women themselves and indeed everybody benefits enormously when women have choices. If Evbhakavbokun had a choice, she would have remained in her father's ruling cabinet and the result might have been positive for all.

So far we have tried to argue that a study of Rotimi's plays can be an excursion in gender relations/imbalance and not merely a representation of historic and mythic stories. In as much as the paper does not seek to disprove fatalism as one causative factor in the historical tragedies, the doom on the tragic heroes have been enhanced by the discriminatory gender relations in the plays. We assert that Odewale's tragedy is gravely boosted by the tradition of bequeathing a surviving wife to her husband's successor which makes him invariably marry his mother just as the vacuum created by Evbakhavbokun's exit adversely affects Ovonramwen's political relations afterwards. Kurunmi's extreme posture of not recognising women in his pursuits earns him an ignominious end where some female instinct and wise advice might have, at least, mitigated his own mistakes. As the resources latent in the women in these patriarchal worlds are left untapped, the sufferings of the men are multiplied. However *Our Husband Has Gone Mad Again* marks a shift in female figure representation in Rotimi's plays. Here the women refuse to wait for approval but intractably forge ahead till they achieve their goal. It is noteworthy that in this play where a woman places herself quietly at the helm of family affairs, the conflict is resolved and things end comically well for everybody. This shift is a trend in Nigerian drama for even a playwright like Soyinka creates a woman Miseyi to work with Sanda to cause a revolution just as Osofisan has variously valourised female characters in his plays. These all go to prove our point that members of the female gender contain in themselves much more virtue than a patriarchal attitude can perceive yet harnessing those potentials might be one way for the healthy development of society.

Chapter 4

Rethinking the African Woman's Identity

HO Okolocha

LIKE the majority of contemporary women writers in Nigeria, Onwueme continues the literary and dramatic tradition of feminist concern for women's issues. Her plays demonstrate a commitment to exploring the challenges facing modern women in changing times. Thus drama, for her, is an excursion into the issues of gender, feminism, identity, race, history, national and international politics, specifically as they affect women. In *Tell it to Women* she makes statements on the nature of feminism as practised by educated women in Nigeria; she provides an insider's exposition of the identity of the African woman and gives a participant's evaluation of the benefits and consequences of feminism as an ideology adopted by educated Nigerian women. This woman's point of view, dominant in Onwueme's writing and in the creativity of contemporary women writers, is a perspective that has not been adequately provided in the literary output of male writers.

Feminism in Nigerian Literature

In general, the term Feminism is the struggle for the liberation of women and encompasses epistemologies, methodologies, theories and modes of activism that work towards bringing an end to the oppression and subjection of women on different planes: social, economic and political. Historically feminist thought and activity can be divided into two waves. The first wave which began in about 1800 and lasted until the 1930s was largely concerned with gaining equal rights between women and men. In England, Mary Wollstonecraft wrote 'A Vindication of the Rights of Woman' (1792) where she demanded equality and better education for women and made the first sustained critique of the social system that relegated women to an inferior position. In 1869, the popular British philosopher and economist, John Stuart Mill, became outspoken on the subject of equality for women, an unpopular cause at the time. His essay entitled 'The Subjection of Women' sought to shift the law and public perceptions in order to free women from what was virtual slavery, and to allow them to live as individuals. The second wave which began in the late 1960s has continued to fight for equality but has also developed a range of theories and approaches that stress the difference between women and men while drawing attention to the specific needs of women (Encarta). Thus feminism is essentially a western construct that has gained universal acceptance and from which we must expect the diversity and variants that typify the different regions and cultures of the world. For instance, Carole Boyce Davies describes the feminism that is African and which supports the African female consciousness in literature as "not antagonist to... men, but challenges them to be aware of certain salient aspects of women's subjugation" (8-9). This indicates that the essence of feminism in Africa is to extract concessions from the patriarchal structures of society for women.

In literary works, these woman-centred ideologies seek to rectify masculine views that have relegated women to insignificant positions. In her essay, "The Female Writer and her Commitment," Omolara Ogundipe-Leslie asserts that it is the duty of the female writer to correct the misconceptions and rewrite the stereotypes propagated by male writers and give a genuine woman's point of view on the following issues: the woman as a writer, as a woman and as a third world person (10). Similarly, Rachael Koenig suggests that the female writer's presentation of issues (especially the presentation of female subject) may challenge the male writer's presentation of the same subject (10). This is because men and women view things differently and there is no self-identification when a male playwright presents a female character. By providing an insider's view, women writers fill a void, and provide the missing perspective in African literature thereby providing a more balanced picture of their society.

The Nigerian literary scenario now has a rich harvest of female writers who identify with women and speak on their behalf. Nigerian novelist Buchi Emecheta provides a good example of self-identification with the female subject in literary productivity. Chukwuma identifies the central theme in all Emecheta's novels as "woman, the feminine gender of the species of homo sapiens" (3). In her novels, the protest against perceived injustices to the woman in society is unrelenting. Zainab Alkali of Northern Nigeria is also concerned and very preoccupied with issues of the woman in her society. Her novel, *The Stillborn*, presents Li, a visionary woman, who is assertive and individualistic in her pursuits. She embodies the feminist doctrine of independence and self-assertion in the sense that she relies on herself, not on a husband, to fulfill her aspirations.

Among her peers Tess Onwueme has proven to be a committed playwright. Onwueme is eminently a political dramatist for her insistence that power affects every other aspect of society; as Evwierhoma asserts, "Onwueme's plays are committed to highlighting the place of women in the various environments in which they find themselves. Through the ideas pivoted on women in her drama, the feminine ideal is propagated with a view to actualizing it in the society" (125). In *The Broken Calabash* Onwueme treats gender roles in a changing society, the conflict between traditional and western values as it affects the woman and the effort of the modern woman to rise above the imposition of culture. In *The Reign of Wazobia* she discusses female power and leadership demonstrating her belief that her duty as an artist is to chart a new path, speak for the voiceless and bring to the fore those issues that have been kept on the sidelines. Onwueme presents the woman as a visionary leader, capable of transforming society that has been mismanaged by men. Her concern with women issues is such that she devotes an entire play to it. However, in *Tell it to Women,* Tess Onwueme's feminist posture takes a significant deconstructive turn.

Rethinking Feminism and the African Identity

Onwueme's presentation of feminism in *Tell it to Women* points to the fact that Nigerian women and feminism have a contradictory relationship because feminism in the African context continues to be highly contested and problematic. It remains essentially a western doctrine which cannot find total affinity with many areas of African life. Even in this era of extreme westernization and globalization, some scholars - male and female - reject the label entirely, while others display various degrees of acceptance and tolerance but support the inclusion of women in male-dominated spaces. While feminism has been a platform for raising the consciousness of women to the existing conditions in the past and present, and for making them aware of future possibilities, still it continues to receive criticism.

The major criticism leveled against feminism is that it only enforces the western world view and the socio-political processes that emanate from it. In addition, Chandra Mohanty et al point out that western feminist theories have serious political implications for the African woman because it is "inscribed within the relations of power" that place western theories and third world women who adopt it at polar ends (53) of superior and inferior. Mohanty also charges western feminism of depicting male and female relationships as permanently embroiled in adversarial conflict which is not necessarily a characteristic of gender relations in Africa. Apart from the binaries that dominate western discourse, the issue of global sisterhood propagated by western feminists is unrealistic because there is little link between the African woman's experiences and the experiences of those western women. Furthermore, it is also impossible to ignore the fact that racism makes solidarity between African and western women impossible. Although we acknowledge that the marginalization of women existed before colonialism, most writers and critics agree that colonialism escalated it into worse dimensions. In her book, *Recreating Ourselves: African Women and Critical Transformations*, Ogundipe-Leslie identifies colonialism as the first mountain the Nigerian woman has to surmount. She argues that through forms of colonial education, indoctrination and government, the woman was propagated as being behind the man. Excluded from public affairs, and from certain jobs and positions of responsibility (28-30), "they lost their meaningful roles within the old production processes" (28). Similarly, Akachi Ezeigbo argues that

> although the traditional African woman lacked political power... she enjoyed considerable economic power and social influence in her community. The misfortune of the modern Nigerian... woman is that she neither enjoys political nor economic power. Her tragedy is that she has virtually lost out on all counts and finds herself even more marginalized and devalued than her traditional foremothers. (xvi)

These assertions that colonialism enabled men's sense of superiority to grow into huge proportions are easily affirmed in the social thought processes of the western world visible in even the most ordinary things. For example, the English language did not see the possibility of a 'woman' as the chair or director of a company hence the title 'chairman' made no allowances for women. The lexicon is so gendered and male oriented that even the words "woman" and "female" are derived from the masculine nouns 'man' and 'male'. Also the terms 'man' and 'human' are used to signify both sexes when there is no need to specify the gender. Nigerian languages show more gender equity in vocabulary. To buttress this, Zulu Sofola points out that in Igbo and Yoruba languages, a common denominator is used in the constitution of words that represent male and female. For example, in Igbo, the word for child, nwa, is used as a root word as in nwa-oke for male and nwa-anyi for female. In Yoruba, it is rin - okunrin (male) and obirin (female). And to refer to both gender inclusively (human), it is madu (Igbo) and enia (Yoruba). There is no hint of the male chauvinism that is enshrined in the English language (53). English society further placed the home as the most respectable place for the middle class woman. One of the most noticeable of its western gendered traditions is the switching of names for the woman when she marries. The woman is considered to be a flower, not a worker. For Karl Marx, women are a man's proletariat. In the Bible, the head of every man is Christ; the head of every woman is man. Besides being contradictory to African cultural norms and attitudes, feminism as depicted by Onwueme in *Tell it Women* also contradicts itself in several ways as adequate illustrations in the text abound.

Onwueme's Feminism in *Tell it to Women*

In this play, Ruth and Daisy - city women and professed feminists - visit Idu to propagate female empowerment. The city women have brought 'Better Life for Rural Women' to rural Idu women in the bid to empower them and bring "light into their lives" (24). These 'better life' city women persuade the rural women to send a representative who will return to the city with them to study the ways of the city and return to teach these new 'better' ways to rural women. Yemoja is chosen to go to the city. However, in the city, Daisy maltreats Yemoja whom she openly scorns as illiterate and, therefore, second-class. Sherifat, Daisy's mother-in-law, is treated with the same hostility and disrespect that Daisy shows Yemoja. Rural women come to realize that Ruth and Daisy have absolutely no interest in improving their lot. Through the actions of these self-proclaimed feminists, one begins to wonder whether their ideology is directed towards anarchic domination of weaker women by their more advantaged sisters rather than centred on liberating all women from strictures, laws, attitudes that have no advantages for them.

Onwueme attempts to point out that feminism as practiced in Europe and America cannot be absorbed completely in Africa, because of the vast differences in culture, values and perceptions that exist between the continents. Through the characters of Ruth and Daisy, Onwueme presents the following as the concept of feminism practiced by these educated Nigerian women, (a) rights and opportunities equal to and surpassing that of men, (b) total freedom of choice for women; the choice to marry, choice to indulge in lesbian relationships or otherwise, choice to procreate etc, (c) western education appears to be a prerequisite for the liberation they preach. Ruth and Daisy do not appreciate anyone without western education. Daisy heaps innumerable insults on Yemoja simply because she is illiterate. Yemoja laments the treatment she gets in Daisy's house: "They treat me like a pig. They say my manners are crude and I am a disgrace to womanhood. That is dirt splashed on my face by my fellow women…" (80).

The brand of feminism illustrated in this text encourages stratification among women and raises a number of questions. Does feminism mean equal rights with men and for women of a certain status and education only? Is education a yardstick for measuring the womanliness of a woman? Is feminism an issue of neo-enslavement for the uneducated woman? To Ruth and Daisy, the rural women are "a disgrace to womanhood" (80), "crude spillover straight from hell" (83), "simplistic minds" (86), " just like a herd of cattle" (87) etc. They do not see the rural women as their equals in any way. Neither do they credit these women with much intelligence. This stratification and inequality also contrasts with the feminist doctrine of equality. Moreover, the modern feminists treat fellow women much worse than the men whom they say they need to be liberated from. Yemoja comes to realize that "… beneath these gold plated words and their worm filled souls" (12), it is another kind of chain: the chain of fellow women and not of men.

Ironically, the man Okei (Daisy's husband) poses no problem in this set up. Yemoja attests that he hasn't contributed to her anguish. She wonders: "who knows when the man will start his own abuse? So far, the man has not bothered with me...." (80) He does not underrate rural women like his wife does. He insists that they are different but not simplistic; to this assertion, Daisy scornfully labels him "defender of the faithful" (116). He advises Daisy against arrogance and condescension in dealing with rural women. He tells her:

Hey, my learned one, if you must win the rural woman over, you must come down from your ivory tower and dialogue with them with respect too. Not this talking down attitude by which you intimidate them from your high towers of academy where you flash neon lights to dazzle them. You must be humble to learn from them. True knowledge humbles but for reckless people like you, knowledge empowers you to the point of intoxication. You have got to change your attitude to appreciate and win the rural women over. (118/119)

Okei could easily have been the true feminist here; he displays the respect and value for women irrespective of status that we should expect from Daisy and Ruth.

A tendency of feminism in *Tell it to Women* is the arrogance and irresponsibility of the educated women. Daisy feels free to go out for business at past midnight to a destination she stubbornly refuses to disclose to her husband. Even age is not a deterrent as she is openly rude and disrespectful to her mother-in-law, Sherifat. Her sense of freedom liberates her from feeling obligated to cook meals for her husband and daughter. Another consequence of feminism seen in this play is the sexual license it confers on the practitioners. In the bid to play men's roles, lesbianism becomes a practice among the feminists. Daisy regards her husband Okei as an enemy and flaunts her lesbian relationship with Ruth before her husband and mother-in-law. Daisy honestly acknowledges to her partner Ruth that this is "radically unconventional". (89). Their extremism only destroys the hitherto manageable relationship in the home and society. Onwueme prods us to wonder if the pursuit of improved advantages for the woman must translate to disadvantages for the man and family. The outrageous acts of Ruth and Daisy in *Tell it to Women* seem like male chauvinism in reverse and negate the essence of the feminist gospel of societal improvement.

The feminist movement as presented in this play does not seem viable in relation to its socio-cultural setting. In fact, it becomes obvious in the text that the brand of feminism practiced by Ruth and Daisy is dangerous to embrace. It is interesting and ironical that the man becomes the only one intent on preserving the home and cultural values which the women seem inclined to destroy. Koko accuses Ruth and Daisy: "You women will be our ruin! You home wreckers! Women, you ruin everything of value to us! You travel to all these strange lands, import new diseases, infect our women and wreck our homes in the name of what?" (63). Feminism as depicted in *Tell it to Women* tends to disintegrate the home. For instance, Daisy aims at being totally independent of both her husband's control and support. Consequently, she does things her way (whether they are good or bad), neither does she care about what her husband does. Okei and Daisy live different lives in the same house, the very essence of marriage which is companionship and communality between couples is eroded. To act as if no one needs the other in the name of freedom obviously does not serve a positive purpose and contrasts with the harmonious co-existence of traditional families. Koko goes on to point out to Ruth and Daisy that we Africans are always on the receiving end of other people's doctrines. He wants to know why we too cannot conquer and impact our own doctrines; he says:

"when the Christians came, they crucified our god and crowned their own. The same with Moslems. And now our women are embracing a new religion: FE-MI-NISM! Ugh!! Must our women take on the ways of women from other lands to become better women?" (64)

In addition, these feminist practitioners would prefer to obliterate and disregard valuable traditional norms and customs as marks of "backwardness". They have absorbed western influences without caution or discretion. Like their imported religions, they are so carried away by the new gospel that they begin to despise tradition. It is noteworthy that both Ruth and Daisy long abandoned their traditional names, language and norms signaling complete alienation from their culture. As a result, they cannot be fully European persons and they have also become strangers to their own world. Hence Sherifat scornfully calls Daisy: "You, woman without tribe or tongue!" (123).

Probably the worst aspect of the feminism as presented by Onwueme is that those who profess it lack belief in the movement or believe in it only to the extent that it affects their personal lives - a movement that is merely a 'fashion' and 'a game' in a money making or profit yielding venture. In a telephone conversation, Daisy enthuses:

Yes... for those of us in government. Yes! We'll make some cool money of course! Yes... Yes... international fame. Yes... of course bringing ourselves to world attention... feminism is the Swiss bank of course! (laughter) But I know your account in Switzerland is breathing... hmm... heavily too! I also know that Ruth will get her promotion on this rural fashion... the new vogue now. Yes... fulfilling the requirements of UN declaration of the Decade for Women. Yes... the government too wants attention and votes for the next election. Yes, buy the people... buy up their conscience. What else? Well who cares what happens afterwards? Who cares what happens to the program after the election? My own money will be resting in some women program... Yes... we're no fools.... And neither is the government. (85)

The above reveals the feminists to be merely hypocrites; they pretend to champion a just cause for the benefit of all women when, in fact, they are only working for personal 'profits' and 'paychecks.' The launching of 'The Better Life Programme' is merely a device, a means to personal ends, for the city women involved. Ruth hopes to get promoted; Daisy hopes to retain her job plus an improved Swiss account. Their hypocrisy is such that they both plan to keep the funds (ten million naira) for the programme to themselves. All the flowery speeches they deliver are mere masks and their promises are empty. It is also noteworthy that the two women do not mind using blackmail. For instance, they insist that the government fund their programme since it will need voters for the next election. This is yet another blemish on feminism.

Onwueme's stance in this play is very different from her unadulterated loyal feminist stance in her previous texts. In this play, she takes the time to expose the loopholes, the problems, inherent in the feminist ideology, and she attacks them from the traditional point of view, the adversarial gender relations it creates, and the hypocrisy that characterizes its major proponents. In addition, feminism is presented as contradictory and irreconcilable with the identity of the woman.

The Social Context of African Feminine Identity

In *Tell it to Women* Onwueme upholds African feminine identity and strength within her social existence thereby forcing us to rethink the feminist doctrine and its implications for the woman. Under the male oriented society depicted in this play, Onwueme creates women who have a correct perception of their own uniqueness, their strengths, weaknesses and areas of need. These women ascribe value to themselves and succeed in extracting immense concessions from their patriarchal society. They achieve this by forcing the society to recognize the areas of power exclusive to women as they work towards improvements in areas where they lack power. For instance, the rural women of Idu show that women are endowed with a natural power that is unique and priceless - motherhood. As no man can become pregnant, the continuity of life in the world can only be ensured by women in all cultures of the world. What feminist women call a burden is rather presented as the pride and ultimate power of African womanhood. Adaku says "for me, motherhood is the ultimate power and I don't know any man yet born of woman who can boast of that power to conceive... I mean create and carry another life" (36). One of the consequences of feminism which Onwueme exposes is its erosion of the natural rights and powers of womanhood in the sense that the freedom of choice characteristic of feminism whereby a woman can decide not to have children in a marriage or not to even marry at all reduces the strength of womanhood in this cultural milieu. The choice not to have children is unacceptable to women in the society where procreation is highly valued and marriage a sign of dignity.

Onwueme presents a traditional African world view rooted in the philosophy of harmony and communalism that upholds a healthy social set up in which both men and women are vital for a healthy and harmonious society. Hence the socio-political situation of rural Idu in the play provides women with several contexts for participation in societal processes and governance. The identity, position and power of woman can be seen in the concept of 'Umuada' (daughters of the clan) who are rightly respected by men and women alike and wield significant influence in the community. There is also the Omu-Adaku (female king) who is solely in charge of the market; not even the male king can challenge her sovereignty in that area. Women are therefore ascribed an identity as managers of the traditional economy. This co-rulership position also features in Onwueme's *The Reign of Wazobia* where the Omu is described as 'her royal highness the king of women.' Her role in the community is summarized when she asks the priest of Ani if he "can snap the finger without the right thumb" (9).

Onwueme takes the trouble to point out that power distribution is indispensable in African world view. In Sherifat's long exhortation to daughter-in-law, Daisy, she points out that male and female roles complement each other. No one can take the place of the other because each role is special and unique. Neither can these different roles be measured in terms of equality because they are not alike. For instance, how can one evaluate equal beauty for the male and female when they have different physical features? Onwueme's authorial voice insists that women have always been valued in Nigerian society. She makes Okeke explain to Yemoja that part of the reason why only male children were sent to school at the initial stage of western education was to protect their precious female children from the strange and unknown entity that was western education. Male children are expected to be able to brave hardships including the unknown. The value for male children is understandable, not because female children are undervalued but because it is the natural course of events for women to marry, take on an extra family identification and inherit a new lineage. The male child is therefore the one who continues the parent's lineage. Even the names given to female children in traditional society illustrate the high value placed on them. Nneka (Mother is Supreme), Ona (precious stone), Adaku (the daughter that brings wealth), Nwanyibuife (a daughter is priceless).

It is worthy of note that rural Idu women so accept and are comfortable with their identity as women that they hold on to and continue to defend their traditional roles and perceptions of womanhood in the face of Ruth and Daisy's flamboyant existence. Faced with an alternative way of existence, they have the confidence of self-awareness that enables them choose what is best for them. Onwueme's loud authorial voice seems to advocate a feminism that retains the best ideas in traditional life. *Tell it to Women* implies that the brand of feminism we need should be one that embraces only ideas in westernization that are profitable to indigenous lifestyles as well as providing improved advantages for the woman. That Onwueme's authorial voice condemns the activities of Ruth and Daisy implies that she would prefer the new feminist woman to discard ideas that do not improve family life and the society as a whole.

In conclusion, we aver that Onwueme is definitely feminist in outlook as majority of her plays testify. Plays like *Legacies, The Reign of Wazobia, The Broken Calabash* and *A Hen Too Soon* are gender-based and gender sensitive. However, in *Tell it to Women,* Onwueme sings a different song. She presents feminism as problematic in African cultural context and advocates a great deal of caution in propagating the modern feminist gospel. She acknowledges the discrepancies within the doctrine, the problems that result from this ideology, and the inappropriate nature of some of its ideas. She advises that ideologies which do not contribute positively to the individual and the society should be embraced with caution. In addition, Onwueme validates the identity of traditional African women. She presents their uniqueness, their strengths and areas of need. She also applauds the self-perception that enables them to identify and withstand the force of negative winds of change. Her argument is that feminist doctrine and awareness must acknowledge and accommodate traditional gender sensibilities, values and needs in order to be useful in society. As Okei says to his wife Daisy,

You feminists may need to reconsider your politics of confrontation and oppositionality; your Cartesian ideology of this or that. Your binary logic of EITHER, OR cannot stand in a world like Idu ... where everything is related and complementary: man AND woman, good AND evil; night AND day etc. Where you envision opposites, they envision difference and complimentarity. That is fundamental if you must enter and capture the mind of Idu (119-120).

It becomes too clear that women's interests, aims and problems have to be addressed within specific contexts and with the awareness of differences. Onwueme indicates that the appropriate articulation of one's self and circumstance is a prerequisite for identifying the problems that afflict women in society and pointing the way to appropriate solutions. She therefore advises the use of caution and discretion in adopting foreign ideologies. This revisionist posture on feminism marks an important shift from the usual stance of her previous works.

Chapter 5

The Conflicts of Fall and Osammor

O Jegede

THE ambiguous portraiture of female characters by some male writers and the phallic nature of men's writings has been a matter of concern to female writers in Africa. From Elechi Amadi's sympathetic portraiture of Ihuoma in The Concubine, to the cowering wives of Okonkwo in Chinua Achebe's Things Fall Apart and more realistic portraits by Ngugi Wa Thiong'o, Sembene Ousmane, Ola Rotimi and Ayi Kwei Armah, the story keeps changing (Kolawole 94). At the early stage, in the African literary scene, most male writers were too preoccupied about themselves to remember women while the few writers like Cyprian Ekwensi presented them in negative images as prostitutes, mistresses, mothers and docile wives incapable of any intellectual exercise.

The battle against the misrepresentation of women is not a battle of the genders as the attempts made by male and female writers in Africa at countering traditional stereotypical representation of women have confirmed this position. It looks at two female writers whose portraiture of women contrast in two of their writings. In

The Beggars' Strike, Fall unwittingly portrays women in less than positive light. It is observed that her attempt to counter previous misrepresentations of women, to a large extent, re-emphasizes the female stereotype by giving voice to the various opinions and oppressions men perpetuate in society. On the other hand, Osammor's portraiture of women in The Triumph of the Water Lily puts forward a positive picture of modern African womanhood. In explicating the selected novels, the paper criticizes writings which demean the value and intelligence of women and calls for more positive portraits which will counter previous misrepresentation of women.

In Womanism and African Consciousness, Kolawole articulates various portraits of women by male writers. While condemning Wole Soyinka's ambivalence, she applauds Akinwumi Isola's and Ola Rotimi's positive female characterization among others. She insists that some women writers portray women in more derogatory images than men and advises that battle lines should not be drawn between the genders.

The need to counter these layers of distortion and misrepresentation has given impetus to diverse reactions from women writers. Women writers have made attempts at writing back, correcting and negotiating such portraits and presenting a better image of women. Their writings, in the last two decades, have countered misrepresentations and recreated the image of womanhood in different ways. Thus more women writers and critics are trying to upstage the gender codes that have promoted male domination of the power structure and its representation in literary works. Explicating the novels of Buchi Emecheta, Mariama Ba and Aminata Sow Fall, Aduke Adebayo praises the efforts of these writers for rejecting the roles of "slaves, wives, mothers and mistresses" (53) which society had designed for them.

A reading of both Aminata Sow Fall's The Beggars' Strike and Stella Ify Osammor's The Triumph of the Water Lily shows how the authors interrogate the marriage institution, counter the misrepresentation of the woman and show some of the options available to her. Helen Cousin's discussion of marriage in fiction in the essay "Submit or Kill Yourself...Your Two Choices" focuses on more common representations of "wives who find that they cannot remain in marriages without equality and autonomy" (106). However, The Beggars' Strike and The Triumph of the Water Lily provide alternatives to the issue of oppression in marriage.

The Beggars' Strike is Fall's second novel; it is a story of conflict, selfishness, abuse of office and marital acrimony. At the centre of these is Mour Ndiaye of the Department of Health and Hygiene mandated to clear the streets of beggars who roam and harass innocent citizens. They had constituted a menace to the economy of the fictive Republic:

...white people especially, are beginning to take an interest in the beauty of our country. These people are called tourists you know in the old days these white people came to rob and exploit us, now they visit our country for a rest and in search of happiness. (17)

In executing this assignment, Mour Ndiaye and his department engage in a serious conflict with the beggars who remain adamant until one of them is crushed on the streets. The department succeeds, through the use of force, in evacuating the beggars from the streets. Not long after, Mour nurses the ambition to become vice president of the Republic. His marabout, Kiki Bokoul, advises him to slaughter a bull and divide it into seventy-seven portions which must be distributed to battu-bearing beggars. This leads him to make frantic efforts at bringing the beggars back. Mour requests Keba Dabo, his assistant, to do this. Keba refuses because Mour's personal interest conflicts with national interest. Mour therefore personally tries to bring the beggars back on the streets, and in the conflict that ensues, the beggars outmanoeuvre him. This shatters Mour's dream.

Ironically, the same fact of the beggars' disability becomes their source of power. Rather than roam and beg for their needs, they now accept gifts by their own terms. The leader of this group is Salla Niang, a woman "with plenty of guts" (Fall 8). From this setting and portraiture of Mour at work, the novel provides the necessary background for the portraiture of Mour at home. The story continues as Mour's political ambitions create more tension and conflict at home. However, the home setting serves as the launching pad for an x-ray of women in polygamous marriage settings.

The novel reflects the imbalances between men and women – such imbalances that may occur about selecting who to marry and how to remain married. The author presents women characters some who are able to overcome stereotypes and others who are not. The three prominent female characters in the novel are the women in Mour's life: Lolli, Sine and Rabbi. They contest their stereotyping in different ways, and exhibit different levels of consciousness: Lolli, his first wife is the submissive, passive, self-sacrificing woman who negotiates, but could not overcome stereotyping, while Sine his second wife is the radical, modern wife who refuses stereotyping. Rabbi his daughter is an unmarried revolutionary with lots of ideas.

The Beggars' Strike portrays the man as the sole authority in marriage. Mour dictates the social roles of his wives and tries to silence and confine them. Polygamous marriage is presented in this novel as a way of establishing men's authority over women, constraining the movement of women and ensuring man's easy movement in the harem. Lolli, the first wife has been married to Mour for twenty four years and all through the years, she "wore herself to a shadow to keep the home going decently on the smell of an oil rag" (31). Like a typical African woman she carries the "burden of the family's survival much more than is generally appreciated" (Kolawole 29). She is relegated to the traditional domestic sphere. When Mour's economic position improves and he is economically empowered, he takes another wife called Sine. When Mour informs Lolli, about his decision to marry another wife, the initial disappointment and shock exhibited by her are expressed in this verbal invective:

What! And you tell me to keep quiet into the bargain you ungrateful wretch! You bastard! You liar! You want me to shut up, do you! Twenty four years of marriage!

You were nothing, nothing but a miserable beggar! And I worked my fingers to the bone, and now you want to share everything you've got with another woman, thanks to my patience and my work, and everything that you got since with my assistance. You ungrateful wretch! You guttersnipe! You liar! You men are all the same, Guttersnipe! Shameless creature! Oh!... I should have suspected this. (31)

Mour's attempt to silence his wife even when she hurts is part of the attempt to make her conform to the passive and submissive stereotype of a wife; and is also part of the misconceived idea that men shape discourse. Being vocal and able to give expression to one's feelings and emotions as Lolli tries to do is a means of resisting oppression. As it is also seen, Lolli's productive labour is not appreciated. With her husband showing blatant insensitivity to her contributions in the relationship, she feels 'used', 'dumped' and frustrated. However, after days of frustration, Lolli succumbs to pressures from family and friends. The novel emphasizes the notion that men dictate social conventions, commonly held beliefs and attitudes when Lolli's father says: "You must know that if Mour divorces you, you will be covered with shame .... Mour is your husband. He is free. He does not belong to you" (33).

The decision to remain in the marriage is not a willing choice. It is informed by the fear of rejection by society. More often than not, women who remain and tolerate unpleasant marriages do so because of what people would say. In line with William Althusser's observation we can identify family and culture as structures which control people's choices and enforce patriarchy (Barry 165). When one's choices are conditioned by culture like Lolli's, one is tricked into believing that (s)he has freedom of choice. Besides, Lolli's low level of education and economic powerlessness to our mind, are further responsible for the fear she exhibits and the decision she takes: "Rabbi, my child if I left this house today, my parents would curse me…I'd have no work, I'd be alone, and what would I do with you children" (34).

Meanwhile Mour's political status improves; his power derives from his wealth and his wife, who had stopped working because of her husband's improved wealth, is stripped of her economic power. The situation enforces her to remain in the unpleasant marriage. Her helplessness and subsequent dependency on her husband are part of the misconceptions that women are incapable of generating wealth. This power structure creates the notion that for women, marriage is the designated route to economic stability, and to remain stable, a woman must remain in marriage; whereas stability in marriage requires more than just remaining as a figure head. Thus, Lolli is trapped and constrained on all sides: socially, economically, psychologically and educationally. Mour's second wife, Sine, appears to have more freedom than Lolli. She smokes and drinks even when Mour forbids. She is a modern wife with second wife syndrome of being the husband's favorite. After asking for Mour's hand in marriage, she discards Mour's stereotyping of her and resists his feminine construct of her:

If you think I'm prepared to be stuck here like a piece of furniture and receive your orders and your prohibitions, then you're making a mistake! I'm a person not a block of wood!.. No! I'm your wife so treat me like a wife... Monsieur disappears for days on end and when he reappears its to start giving me orders! Oh! No, Mour! You can do that to your Lolli, but I'm no sheep. (95)

Sine rejects her traditional and domestic roles and thus distinguishes herself from Lolli, the conservative and dogmatic wife. The Sine/Mour relationship demystifies, disrupts, deconstructs and subverts the established male-dominant/female-submissive dynamic which is characterized in Lolli. However despite Sine's rejections of Mour's orders, she is as unfulfilled as Lolli. The Beggars' Strike portrays the woman as a subject of repression, a sexual subordinate, objectified and transformed into a source of desire that alternately tempts and pleases man. It interrogates the marriage institution and confirms it to be a prison. Through Mour's daughter, Rabbi, the novel problematises the marriage mode which requires unquestioned submission.

Rabbi is a revolutionary with lots of ideals. Her ideas run counter to conventional gender construction. She is the emerging educated revolutionary woman whose ideological position contests the negative stereotyping of women. She expresses herself freely because she is educated and unmarried. Through Rabbi, the novelist, like most contemporary African writers, attempts to redefine marriage and the place of the woman in it. However, Rabbi is antagonistic and individualistic. What she advocates about marriage – divorce – has a tinge of the radicalism of western feminism. The fact that Rabbi remains unmarried makes her suggestions only idealistic.

On the other hand Salla Niang, leader of the beggars, is an economically viable woman who built a house with the proceeds of her begging. She has a firm grip on her husband and other male characters in the novel, dictating the path for them to follow. This untraditional role-reversed portrait puts her in a number of competent social functions. Thus the characters in the novel are representations of different options to oppression in marriage – to be submissive, rebellious or idealistic.

On her part Stella Ify Osammor's The Triumph of the Water Lily presents the woman's struggle from an African context in a rather interesting way. The novel, which is Osammor's first, celebrates womanhood within the framework of wifehood and discusses marriage with all the seriousness that is attached to it in Africa. The seriousness with which marriage is handled in the novel brings to mind the central position given to it in both Africa and in womanist poetics: a male inclusive theory that foregrounds the complementary role of men and women. This is the nucleus of African gender system. Nkem and Odili, the protagonists, have been childless for seven years after marriage. Odili's family therefore pressurises him into marrying again. A new wife named Comfort is taken for him. Nkem, the legal wife chooses to be Odili's mistress and decides to exchange her role as a wife for that of a mistress. She packs out of the home because she would "rather be that (mistress) than a derelict and pitiful wife who is left home dejected and embittered and only in possession of the wedding ring and not the man himself" (11). Unlike Lolli, Nkem negotiates her value. To her, being a mistress is more valuable than being an abandoned wife. Nkem's decision which she believes will enhance her position with Odili and his family is a reaffirmation of some of the misconstrued portraits by writers. Despite Nkem's decision, nothing changes between her and her husband. They remain very much in love with each other (13). Nkem is left to make this choice and give her husband the freedom to satisfy what she considers to be an important need such as childbearing; 'a need which society deems 'fundamental' (17) since childlessness is a dilemma for a woman because as Emecheta sardonically puts it a "woman without children is nowhere"(Mineke Schipper 191). In Osammor's The Triumph of the Water Lily, as in Fall's The Beggar's Strike, plural marriage and childlessness are problematised and universalized:

Marriages get arranged and annulled by families for political and socio-economic reasons and not merely for love. Concubines are arranged to produce heirs if the woman taken in wedlock is unable to beget any. (11)

Osammor interrogates traditional beliefs about marriage and childlessness in marriage. Through the Nkem/Odili relationship, she shows that love in marriage is crucial for childbearing. Despite her childlessness, Nkem is still endeared to Odili. She is treated with love and respect and given fair hearing in the relationship. The plan to get another wife for Odili was told Nkem by Odili's stepmother, Mama Asaba. Not long after, Comfort gets pregnant and Nkem is shattered by the news. This creates a personal crisis to which Odili and Effua, her friends, quickly respond to. Comfort loses the pregnancy and Odili reunites with his wife. Shortly after this, Nkem gets pregnant, travels abroad and later gives birth to a baby boy; experiencing motherhood as a possible and profound role. Performing her reproductive role gives her much satisfaction.

One can infer that although Nkem had been through so many crises and emotional upsets, she still manages to overcome them with courage and grace. The author seems to say that the battles of life are enormous and only the courageous can win. The water lily is the metaphor for Nkem and every woman. Osammor re-emphasizes the importance of motherhood and mothering as necessary steps to marital fulfilment and means to "female identity formation" (Bungaro 67). The climax of the story is when Nkem falls ill and later dies. This stylistic subversion of the stereotype image of the 'mother as carrier of life and eternal nurturer' (69) introduces further tension in the narrative. In pursuance of the author's systematic womanist agenda in the novel, she makes Effua, Nkem's friend view marriage with seriousness. Effua agrees that to reach her fullest potential as a woman, she needs a man: "Marriage is a very serious business Norman, and I would very much want it to last. That is why I want you to please give me some time" (17).

Having lost her childhood sweetheart during the civil war, she is emotionally upset and careful about choosing another partner. When she meets another man who captures her emotions, she takes her time before entering into any relationship with him. The novel reveals that marriage requires commitment and understanding. Her female characters make their choices without being pushed around by men. They are career women who combine many roles. Being a career woman and a responsible wife, friend, daughter and mother are possibilities that the novel emphasizes. For instance, Effua is a successful journalist and so also is her fiancé Norman. Norman even works on the presidential team. Both characters treat each other with respect and love. They relate first as human beings and then as man and woman on equal basis. This underscores the point made by Kolawole that African womanism cannot be separated from humanism. Rather, it seeks to enrich the "female gender through consciousness raising while giving a human touch to the struggle for the appreciation, emancipation, elevation and total self-fulfillment of the woman in positive ways" (204). The female characters in The Triumph of the Water Lily are admirable and are as competent as their male counterparts. They are what Lolli in The Beggars' Strike is not: educated, exposed, and working professional and wealthy women. These qualities enable them to take control of their situation and create the space within which they operate and make choices which affect their lives and those of others. They are liberated and fulfilled individuals who assert power and are sources of liberation – extending freedom to those around them. Indeed the robust portrait of the Effua/Norman and Nkem/Odili relationships stands to correct the African world view of male heroism that is presented by male writers and Aminata Sow Fall in The Beggar's Strike.

Contemporary Nigerian female writings have clearly marked paths of raising African feminine consciousness and resisting any reality that affects or undermines the humanity of women. Thus women become vocal and active arbiters of change; speaking of their gender and to their gender thereby creating a world that is devoid of gender boundaries, one in which people relate as human beings, respecting the views and feelings of one another. While Fall's Lolli and Sine struggle for space and voice, Osammor's characters are visible and audible. Osammor's fiction re-defines and restores the image of women. As she portrays the woman as an agent of change, she refuses the claim that the woman is silent and invisible. These contrastive representations of the modern womanhood by the two female writers seems to justify the opinion expressed by Kolawole that the battle against misrepresentation of women is not necessarily a battle of the genders as some women writers are more ambivalent than men. Fall does not clearly and fully portray women in positive light and her attempt to counter previous misrepresentations of women to a large extent re-emphasizes female stereotypical portraits

Chapter 6

The Women of Ousmane and Dlamini

F I Mogu

SINCE the advent of time and civilization, women have confronted what they perceive to be the male domination of affairs in the human society. According to the African-American feminist critic, May Helen Washington, all facets of the society must conform to the male order before they are adjudged to be correct. However, she reasons that this scenario cannot continue since it is lopsided and punitive against women. She argues for a fairer, egalitarian, non-sex biased society which accords similar rights and privileges to its male and female members alike. In her essay, "The Darkened Eye Restored: Notes Towards a Literary History of Black Women," she opines:

What we have to recognise is that the creation of the fiction of tradition is a matter of power, not justice, and that power has always been in the hands of men mostly white but some black. Women are the disinherited.... Those differences and the assumption that those differences make women inherently inferior, plus the appropriation by men of the power to define tradition, account for women's absence from our written records (Gates 32).

In The Sexual Mountain and Black Women Writers Adventures in Sex, Literature and Real Life, Calvin C. Hernton supports Washington's views and proceeds to show clearly that the male domination of all aspects of life in the society still exists. He reasons that "the complexity and vitality of black female experience have fundamentally been ignored" and that, "black male writing has been systematically discriminating against women" (Hernton 39).

The situation referred to by Washington and Hernton reveals itself in the societies projected by Lucy Dlamini and Sembene Ousmane in Swaziland and the French speaking regions of West Africa respectively. Like in the African-American setting, women begin to emerge from behind the veil of male-based culture to voice their needs and concerns. Initially, they are taken for granted. Conversely, as events unfold, men begin to take them serious and to contend with their yearnings and aspirations.

Dlamini's The Amaryllis is set in Swaziland in the late 1960s and early 1970s. It also forays into neighbouring countries like South Africa, Botswana, and Lesotho. The title of her novel recalls a beautiful, pink-coloured, and sweet scented, but rare flower that grows from a bulbous plant found usually in semi-arid areas. Ousmane's God's Bits of Wood on the other hand, is set in the late 1940s largely in Mali and Senegal, two prominent regions in the former French West Africa. It is essentially about the strike action embarked upon by African workers on the Dakar-Niger Railway Line which spanned thousands of kilometres across different time zones, territories, peoples and cultures. Put simply, "God's bits of wood" means 'children of God the Creator' (Ousmane 62).

Dlamini's novel is about Tana Tanethu and other members of the Mdluli family in their quest to build a strong, economically sound and united family amidst the social chaos and decay of moral values in the Logoba / Mhobodleni / Ka Khoza area resulting from the rural to urban migration and the mushrooming of squatter settlements. These settlements were occasioned by the quest for wage employment at this period in the history of Swaziland, which threatens their efforts. The Amaryllis equally celebrates the establishment of the University of Swaziland fondly referred to as "Mvasi" and the warm reception accorded it by the Swazi nation. Historical figures such as the late King Sobhuza II and Professor S.M. Guma, accord the story some verisimilitude. Thus, the novel is a mixture of fact and fiction, credible and incredible events. The book therefore recalls works such as Felix Mnthali's Yoranivyoto and manifests affinity with God's Bits of Wood in the sense that, as Ousmane's novel recalls and celebrates the 1947/48 Workers' strike the Dakar Niger Railway Strike which outcome uplifted African workers and restored some of their dignity which had been denied them by the French Colonizers. In the Amaryllis, we witness a young woman making choices and determining her future. Viewed against the backdrop of her culture, the heroine of the story appears to be rebelling against the status quo.

Whereas the heroine in Dlamini's novel is Tana, in Ousmane's book it is Penda and a host of other women who ensured the success of the worker's strike embarked upon by their male folk. Penda led the African women on a long, arduous protest march to Dakar the French colonial Capital. In the course of the march and in the entire process of the strike, she was assisted and envisioned by other women like Dieynaba, Ramatoulaye and even the little Ad'jibd'ji and the blind Maimouna.

In God's Bits of Wood as in The Amaryllis, the events unfold over a vast canvass or landscape. The canvass in Ousmane's work is wider and larger that that in Dlamini's book. However, key activities occur within selected locations in the two texts such as Dakar, Thie`s, Bamako, Manzini and the University of Swaziland premises at Kwaluseni. The central point however in the two works is the emergence of the heroes and heroines who actively champion the cause of the ordinary downtrodden people in the society. In this case, we are looking at ordinary women who through dogged determination, commitment and discipline emerge as leaders and spokespersons of their various groups.

The renowned African writer, Ngugi waThiong'o argues in his book of essays, Home Coming, that "the artist must be part of the national struggle" (Ngugi xv). A relevant artist employs his art to educate the present generations of people while charting the future for them. The above ideas are also central in Ousmane's God's Bits of Wood and Dlamini's The Amaryllis. Ousmane portrays a colonial society undergoing transition. The colonized African people of "French West Africa" realise their innate power and potentials through group action. Through the 'Railway Strike, they realise that they could effect a change for the better in their lives. Prior to the strike, many of them did not believe that group coordination of efforts could result in a change for the better in their conditions of living. Dlamini on her part, paints a vivid picture of an emerging nation the Kingdom of Swaziland, with a population that eagerly welcomes the establishment of its premier academic institution the University of Swaziland owing to the people's enthusiasm for knowledge acquisition.

The dominant narrator through whose eyes we witness events in The Amaryllis is Tanethu Mdluli Tana for short. She is the first child and daughter to the Mdlulis. She is an ambitious, disciplined, intelligent, ideal and likeable personality that is also naïve in some instances. Tana is dutiful and completely devoted to her family and to her studies. In the University she falls in love with Reuben a fellow student but refuses to sleep with him. She believes that sexual consummation should come after marriage. Reuben however proceeds to date Sylvia and, in the course of the relationship, impregnates her even though he is not willing to marry her because he believes his real love to be Tana.

Although the society depicted in the story seems to turn a blind eye on Reuben's lack of responsibility over Sylvia's pregnancy and plight, Tana faces a dilemma as she cannot understand why a young man who claims to love her, but has put another lady in the family way and abandoned her in the process, still wants her to marry him. Tana is determined to climb to the top of the academic and career ladders. She is resilient and does not experiment with casual sexual relationships as her younger sister, Zakhe and her bosom friends and schoolmates. She is resolute in her convictions about dating a single man and avoiding sexual intercourse until after marriage. This stance deprives her of her first and only boy friend, Reuben who is impatient to the point that he experiments with a willing girl. Tana's position is at odds with the prevailing trend in the Swazi Society so vividly depicted. She believes the trend to be morally reprehensible. She thus wages a relentless war to sensitise her siblings at home and her friends at school against such a practice. Her posture which stands against the predominant male ordered ethos surrounding her, is credible and realistic, but appears strange and weird in the existing social parlance. However, she is the voice of reason, a visionary whose actions and beliefs serve to warn against the consequences of promiscuity as manifested in the contemporary society. Tana Mdluli is therefore a suitable role model for today's youth in our HIV AIDS' devastated world.

In God's Bits of Wood, a strike situation involving local African workers demanding equal labour rights and fairer treatment from their French Colonial employers serves to mobilize and enlighten both men and women to united action and team work against their oppressors and exploiters. For instance, it is during the strike that, contrary to their traditional role as housewives, women are allowed to attend and address a political meeting in a society where the very idea is "unfamiliar and disturbing." We therefore realise "how many traditional beliefs are being swept aside by the turbulence of the strike" (Wilfred 178).

The Dakar-Niger Railway Strike brings about a situation where men become increasingly dependent on women:

The days passed, and the nights. In this country, the men often had several wives, and it was perhaps because of this that, at the beginning, they were scarcely conscious of the help the women gave them. But soon they began to understand that, here, too, the age to come would have a different countenance. When a man came back from a meeting, with head bowed and empty pockets, the first things he saw were always the unfired stove, the useless cooking vessels, the bowls and gourds ranged in a corner, empty. Then he would seek the arms of his wife, without thinking, or caring, whether she was the first or the third. And seeing the burdened shoulders, the listless walk, the women became conscious that a change was coming for them as well...And the men began to understand that if the times were bringing forth a new breed of men, they were also bringing forth a new breed of women. (Ousmane 53-54)

Penda, a fearless female, organises a march with other women in support of the Workers' Strike. She subsequently emerges as a foremost leader of the march by African women from Thie`s to Dakar. In the course of the strike she makes a speech at one of their meetings. The speech confirms her leadership status:

I speak in the name of all of the women, but I am just the voice they have chosen to tell you what they have decided to do. Yesterday we all laughed together, but for us women this strike still means the possibility of a better life tomorrow. We owe it to our selves to hold up our heads and not give in now. So we have decided that tomorrow we will march together to Dakar (254 -255).

The Amaryllis depicts a situation where the protagonist, Tanethu Mdluli's unique personality emerges. Her male friend, Reuben takes her out to the lawn for a chat soon after they meet at the University. In the course of the chat we observe her resolute position on issues such as dating and courtship. Reuben ventures thus:

'Tana,' ...'I would like to know you better, and maybe you and I

could be friends in a special kind of w...' However, Tana responds:

'Not so fast Reuben, ... 'we scarcely know each other yet' (Dlamini 70)

At this point, Tana patiently listens to Reuben a he intimates her with his family background. Once in a while she interjects to elicit more information from him. It is only when he has finished telling her his background that she responds fully by letting him know about her. When, much later, Reuben raises the issue of pre-marital sex, Tana resolutely opposes the idea. Tana's other name is Busisiwe which literally means "we are blessed to have you" (57). Therefore, she must live up to her billing. At the start of her University programme, her parents emphasise this point to her:

'My child, Tana,' Father said, turning to me, 'your mother and I don't know how to thank you for being such a blessing to this family. You have truly lived up to your name, Busisiwe "we are blessed to have you" which your mother gave you. Your mother and I feel truly blessed for having such a child.'

'We also trust that you'll continue to heed our advice while you're at that place of higher learning, which we have been warned, can destroy a child morally. Also, do not forget to read your Bible.'

'So, my child, ... we, in turn, will keep you in our prayers, beseeching the Almighty to keep you on His straight and narrow path (57- 58).

This parental advice and exhortation further strengthens Tana's convictions about her future and her leadership role both in her family and in the larger society. Hence, in her rapport with friends and schoolmates, this resolute commitment, which seems to be solitary in her neighbourhood, stands out conspicuously. It also sustains her when Reuben, her boyfriend, attempts to blackmail her into engaging in pre-marital sex with him through his carnal and superficial relationship with Sylvia a girl adjudged to be wayward. Tana's bosom friends and school mates, Julie and Patience try to persuade her to revise her stern stance regarding casual sex, but she remains committed to her resolution against it. Julia admonishes Tana:

'You know, Tana,' ... 'I wouldn't be your true friend if I didn't give you my honest opinion. Reuben loves you, and I've not the slightest doubt that if you revised your stand on certain expectations in a relationship between two people who love each other, he would dump that ntji...'

'No, Tana. I'm telling the truth. Reuben's using Sylvia for what he can get while waiting for you to change your mind (94).

However, Tana does not change her attitude or waver in her tough stance. She instead sulks and devotes all her energies to her studies in a bid to surmount the emotional set-back:

In the succeeding days and weeks, I felt as conspicuous as an aching tooth, knowing that most people were aware that my relationship with Reuben, begun with such promise (though Bemona, the malicious would call it pride) had been nipped in the bud. To stifle the pain I buried myself in my books, deriving deep satisfaction when each assignment was returned with nothing less that a B grade and very warm comments from my lecturers. At weekends I escaped to my home to breathe fresh air. Meanwhile, Reuben himself had kept his distance since the Sunday following my discovery. After church he had approached me but I had frozen his steps in mid-stride by hissingly telling him to get lost. And from then on, I never looked back. I was disillusioned and bleeding inside, but I refused to give either him or the onlookers the satisfaction of seeing me waver (98).

In God's Bits of Wood, Penda's speech at the strikers' meeting in Thie's energizes other women into positive action as they decide to march to Dakar to vent their anger and frustration at the French Colonial exploitation of African workers. It is even acknowledged that, "it was the first time in living memory that a woman had spoken in public in Thie`s,..." (255). Ibrahim Bakayoko who is viewed as the 'strength' and 'soul' of the strike, lends firm support to the women in their planned march. Bakayoko and Lahhib are regarded as the 'soul' and 'brain' of the Dakar Niger Railway Strike respectively. Bakayoko tell the other strikers:

'We have no right to discourage anyone who wants to strike a blow for us,' he said brutally. 'It may be just that blow that is needed. If the women have decided, all that is left for us to do is help them. I move that the delegates from Dakar leave immediately to warn the local committee of their arrival... (255- 256)

True to Bakayoko's reading, the march from Thie`s to Dakar proceeds and succeeds. It thus becomes the lethal blow which serves to alert the French Colonizers to the firm resolve of the African Strikers to attain their objectives of having all the demands met. The solidarity exhibited by the women in their march to the colonial headquarters strengthens the strike and adds fervour to it. The workers refuse to return to work under the old working conditions and the strike drags on and degenerates into what Hadrame the shopkeeper describes as "a war of eggs against stones" (65). The authorities cut off supplies of food and water in a desperate and cruel attempt to force the strikers back to work.

In the resulting hardships and confrontation with agents of the colonial authorities, many people lose their lives. Those who survive suffer untold hardships that extenuate their endurance and this brings out the worst traits in some individuals, while it also reveals the best, but hidden attributes in others. Still, the workers remain adamant and the strike lingers on. In the end they win as the French Colonial Railway Company accedes to the Strikers' demands. A foremost leader of the Strike, Lahbib, sends a telegram from Dakar which confirms the end of the Strike: "Conditions accepted.Strike terminated.Return to work tomorrow…" (320).

It is plain that, whereas in The Amaryllis, Tana Mdluli is a moral voice for Swazi women on crucial social issues that affect all women, Penda and other females in God's Bits of Wood actively join their menfolk in an economically driven battle against colonial, capitalist exploitation to regain dignity for Africans. In the process the women break new grounds as they begin to make themselves heard and felt poignantly in public meetings for the first time in their society. Dlamini's novel voices opposition to some long-established, male-based practices in the Swazi society as exemplified in the responses of the heroine, Tana to these manifestations, while Ousmane's book shows African women in a colonial and exploitative situation pooling their energies and ideas together to wrest the initiative from their foreign oppressors as a step towards redefining themselves and charting the future for oncoming generations regarding the usefulness of team work. To corroborate the story, Ousmane remarks in his Author's Note on the Dedication Page of the novel:

The men and women who, from the tenth of October, 1947, to the nineteenth of March, 1948, took part in this struggle for a better way of life owe nothing to anyone: neither to any "civilizing mission" nor to any parliamentarian. Their example was not in vain. Since then, Africa has made progress (v).

History has revealed that Ousmane was among the strikers. Even though the story is told with some fictional undertones in a novelised form, the strike did occur within the dates stated above. And, the African strikers won a sweet victory which serves as a lesson till today. Ousmane's statement above serves as a backdrop to the revolutionary import of God's Bits of Wood and goes a long way to give the Railway Strike much credence and place it within the framework of a historical milieu. The author employs this propitious historical framework to present exemplary characters and pursue nearly all of his favourite themes of anti-exploitation, anti-colonialism and pro-Africanness (Pan Africanism) themes espoused and propagated by the Negritude Movement. Ousmane is therefore an Africanist who is fully committed to the ideals of black consciousness or the beauty of the African cultural heritage.

A close reading of The Amaryllis reveals that, like Ousmane, Dlamini equally cherishes and advocates this Africanist consciousness. Accordingly, she projects key characters in her novel who set the tone for other people to follow. For instance, she vehemently condemns and renounces some emerging tendencies: the renegade western habits of loose living, casual attitudes and the appropriation by females of male clothes. These are practices that run counter to the traditional African heritage of closely-knit family subsistence. As Tana Mdluli is ready to depart for further studies at the University, her father remarks:

While I cannot say all daughters should follow their mothers' examples, at least I can ask you to do exactly that. My child, don't like your prodigal sister, deprive us of the joy of one day giving you away in marriage to a deserving young man, and of presenting us soon after with grandchildren, all begotten within a marriage sanctioned by the church. I, therefore, ask you to keep away from all those alcohol-drinking and cigarette-smoking young men.

'This country is changing before our eyes. Certain behaviours that we thought belonged to big cities like Jozi or Thekwini have now been brought here. For example, I have even seen some of your age mates walking around in trousers. Again, we don't expect you, once you are out of our sight, to begin dressing like a harlot. Trousers belong to men. Why indeed should women want to wear trousers when we men never long to be seen in a skirt?'

'So, my child, I don't expect you to defile your father's house by coming here wearing trousers. You are not a man nor have I seen any indication of the harlot in you ....' (Dlamini : 58).

Ousmane and Dlamini employ literature to propagate their cultural ideals. Dlamini's heroine, Tana remains steadfast throughout the story. She heeds her parents' advice. Ousmane's females led by Penda energize their menfolk with a supportive protest march from Thie`s to Dakar in their bid to ensure a successful strike. Both writers harness history by recreating action and recalling events which occurred in the past to spur other generations to follow the appropriate paths by making the right choices in life. Essentially then, the two texts act as vehicles for far-reaching and progressive social change. The characters in the two novels embark on a journey of change for the better in their various societies.

Chapter 7

Female Subjectivity in Achebe's Novels

O Ojeahere

IN her article, "Sisterhood: Political Solidarity between Women," bell hooks explains that the concept of "sisterhood" was a development that was fundamental to the idea of "common oppression" (396) developed by feminists. According to hooks, because the female group is oppressed, women need to work against the conditioning of patriarchy. She writes:

Male supremacist ideology encourages women to believe we are valueless and obtain value only by relating to or bonding with men. We are taught that our relationships with one another diminish rather than enrich our experience. We are taught that women are natural enemies, that solidarity will never exist between us because we cannot, should not, and do not bond with one another. We have learned these lessons well. We must unlearn them if we are to build a sustained feminist movement. We must learn the true meaning and value of sisterhood. (396)

hooks points out that because of differences and implicit or explicit discrimination in terms of race and class, the women's movement in the US has failed to present a united front. She suggests that for these women to unite and achieve their goals, they need to struggle to overcome these divisions within their own ranks.

Implicitly responding to hook's argument in "Beyond Gender Warfare and Western Ideologies: African Feminism for the 21st Century," Anthonia Akpabio Ekpa acknowledges that as with US feminism, the concept of African feminism aims to provide woman with a sense of self-identity. While she admits that feminism in Africa is yet to be fully received, but asserts, "if practiced with an African bias and respect for African values, feminism promises to be enlightening and acceptable as its tenets prove" (31). She suggests that attention also needs to be given to the strengths of women's lives that have not particularly been highlighted by writers. "Rather than promote the stereotype of the antagonistic woman," Ekpa suggests, "writers must explore co-operation, love, assistance, and understanding among women" (35). For Ekpa, then the difficulty of achieving pan-African feminism is not so much embodied in disputes between race and class, but rather in the presentation of woman by feminists.

Despite the hurdles these critics see as confronting feminism today, both hooks and Ekpa seek ways of advocating for women's rights in order to improve women's condition through unification of the women's movement. Chinua Achebe's novels No Longer at Ease and Anthills of the Savannah may be seen as seeking this same end considering the way his female characters have fared in their relation with one another and in society more generally. This paper reveals that, in terms of gender, Achebe points at modern colonial lifestyles as offering only a veneer of older cultural values, arguing, in chorus with women like Ekpa and hooks, that in order to fight the seemingly oppressive structures that have traditionally discriminated against them, women must disregard their diversity and embrace unity. By their solidarity and unity, women can resist the powerful conditioning of patriarchy.

In African Politics in Comparative Perspective Goran Hyden discusses the patterns of conflict, and reveals two types: manifest and latent conflicts. He explains that there are human casualties in manifest conflicts because of its fierce nature, but says that is not the case with latent since they are "hidden in societal cleavages" (191). Hyden goes on to say that vertical and horizontal cleavages are the categories of societal cleavages. While he claims that religion, race, and ethnicity are the fundamental reasons for vertical cleavages, he asserts that the desire for economic manipulation of resources results in horizontal. Thus he reveals that "class" can be traced to horizontal cleavages (191). The fascinating thing is that this description of conflict is prevalent in Achebe's two narratives where his characters are immersed in both types of conflicts. The affinity of his characters will show the different classes these females belong to and perhaps how these conflicts impact their lives.

In examining the two stories, it is evident that the central female characters of the two novels, Clara and Beatrice, are depicted to play active roles in the lives of their men. They are the backbone of their male counterparts, making crucial decisions in the face of difficulty and misfortune, and assume responsibility for such resolution even when their men are incapacitated. Both are part of the professional working-class, and depicted as independent, a change from the usual domestication of women who are reliant on their men. While Clara is an Assistant Nursing Sister in a government hospital, Beatrice is an Assistant Secretary in the Ministry of Finance. Both are educated abroad and have foreign degrees: Clara studied nursing in England. Beatrice has a first-class honors degree in English from Queen Mary College, University of London. Both are strong-minded: Clara makes a decision to finally sever her relationship with Obi when it dawns on her that he is too weak to stand up to his parents. Likewise Beatrice refuses to play the subordinate role that Sam, the President, expects her to play to the American journalist. Both are fiancées: Clara is Obi's fiancée. Beatrice is Chris' fiancée. Both are supportive, thoughtful, and take initiative: Clara loans Obi her money; Beatrice tries to reconcile three warring friends: Ikem, Chris, and Sam.

However the portrait we see of the other female characters, Hannah, Agatha, and Elewa reveals the different class structures of these women. Hannah is semiliterate; she can read so she must have had a bit of the village-missionary education considering the historical period of her time. She is a wife and mother, loves Obi her child, loves story-telling as we see in the folktale she tells Obi, is a no-nonsense woman, as she demonstrates when she kills the village priest's goat when it eats her yams. And she is a zealous and devout woman in her faith –one of the converted female Christians in Umuofia. Agatha, on the other hand, is single, illiterate (nothing much is disclosed about her education), maid to Beatrice and therefore presumably of a lower class, and she is religious – given the picture of her preaching acts and church attendance. Elewa in her own case is semiliterate, is a sales girl, and oversees a lower-class stand as the daughter of a market woman who lives in a one-bedroom apartment. She is also Ikem's girlfriend and eventually mother of his child.

Achebe's No Longer at Ease demonstrates the conflict that women must overcome in addressing both gender and class disputes through the clash of personalities represented by Clara and Hannah. Clara and Hannah are the dominant people in the life of Obi, Achebe's male protagonist, and they belong to different class structures. While Clara is a symbol of the modern woman, Hannah represents duty to tradition. Obi is described as a young man who has a bright future ahead of him. But because of a bribery accusation, he appears before a magistrate to answer the allegation. As S.A. Khayyoom notes, "the novel is not about the crime, but about the compelling circumstances that lead to Obi's fall" (61). But at the moment when Obi appears to answer these accusations, neither of these female protagonists plays an active role in his life, as his mother has passed away and Clara has left his life. The narrator explains that these "two events following closely on each other had dulled [Obi's] sensibility and left him a different man, able to look words like 'education' and 'promise' squarely in the face" (NLAE 2). Without traditional Umuofia, represented by his mother, and modern woman, represented by Clara –

indeed without the presence of women altogether-- there are no complications in the ideal of education and promise. In An Introduction to the African Novel: A Critical Study of Twelve Books, Eustace Palmer comments on "Achebe's social concern and his terse, ironic, lucid, unpretentious style. His scintillating wit, which is itself the index of his objectivity and maturity of outlook, is everywhere apparent" (71). Indeed through Achebe's "objectivity," the variance in class and gender is depicted in the use of satire. Hannah's life reveals a glimpse of the role of the woman in traditional Igbo culture and her reason for opposing Obi's proposed wedding plans. When Obi goes to the village to see his parents, their reaction to news of his impending marriage to Clara is unsurprising given their different castes within Ibo tradition. Even for Obi's father, the idea is simply ridiculous. He explains what the consequences of Obi's action might be:

Osu is like leprosy in the minds of our people. I beg of you, my son, not to bring the mark of shame and of leprosy into your family. If you do, your children and your children's children unto the third and fourth generations will curse your memory. . . . You will bring sorrow on your head and on the heads of your children. Who will marry your daughters? Whose daughters will your sons marry? Think of that my son. (NLAE 133-34)

As John Njoku also points out, the issue of Osu is one of social stratification which has been defined by scholars as "a cult slave, a living sacrifice, untouchable, an owner's cult, a slave of the deity, a sacred and holy being" (33). We notice that none of the arguments Obi employs can persuade his father to accept his choice of a wife. A social boundary between the supposedly freeborn and the outcast exists so they cannot mingle. For Isaac to have been adamant about the subject –which would seem to contradict the supposed "democracy" of his adopted faith– shows the seriousness of the issue. And yet Obi predicts this reaction.

For Obi, Hannah's reaction is more shocking than that of his father. David Carroll notes in Chinua Achebe that the "instinctual opposition of [Obi's] mother is more disturbing even than that of his father because it cannot be explained and discussed" (83). Hannah thinks Obi's marriage to Clara would signify the end of her life, especially because she believes she and Obi have a special relationship. She tells Obi that his marrying an outcast and bringing disgrace upon the family would be unbearable for her. It is a wonder why she, who has always been more open-minded, eager to blend cultural traditions with new ones, is even more unwavering about his intended marriage than his father. We also wonder if the woman has found an avenue to exercise her own power, which perhaps has been denied her by her husband and the community. For instance, Achebe offers us a glimpse into this oppression when Obi is at home with his parents, and the entire family gathered together for prayer:

Obi's mother sat in the background on a low stool. The four little children of her married daughters lay on the mat by her stool. She could read, but she never took part in the family reading. She merely listened to her husband

and children. It had always been like that as far as the children could remember. She was a very devout woman, but Obi used to wonder whether, left to herself, she would not have preferred telling her children the folk-stories that her mother had told her. In fact, she used to tell her eldest daughters stories. But that was before Obi was born. She stopped because her husband forbade her to do so. (NLAE 57-58)

Even Obi suspects that Hannah has been deprived of what she enjoys to dutifully serve her husband. Her subservient role in her home may account for her using her power against Clara, even threatening suicide should he proceed with his plan. Hannah's action is indeed baffling because one would have thought that, as a woman, she might be more understanding and accommodating, and would be willing to find a common ground of agreement in welcoming Clara into the household —especially because of the seemingly oppressive position of women in her society. But Achebe's point is that oppression begets oppression: when an opportunity arises for Hannah to use what little power she possesses, she employs it as a weapon to oppose Clara, a woman like herself, instead of turning against the system that has oppressed her. Her goal to uphold this Umuofia tradition is not necessarily the right action, but she sees Clara as the only one over whom she can exercise her dominance, an opportunity rarely afforded her. In Hannah's attitude, we perceive in Umuofia's traditions race hierarchies, caste hierarchies, and gender hierarchies —all of which are repressive, and all of which reinforce the others.

We observe these repressive structures when Clara and Obi return home to Nigeria after their experience abroad. During their boat ride from England, when she and Obi first meet, Clara displays her nursing skills by administering medicine to her fellow travelers, (Obi among them), who are seasick. She is Achebe's symbol of modern female independence, with which Obi, with his modern European education, is initially comfortable. But as Achebe demonstrates, Clara's position changes as soon as they reach Lagos. There, she is relegated to the role of Obi's girlfriend: she cleans the house, cooks for him, and sleeps with him. Not much is said again about her professional training and Achebe focuses more on Clara as a sexual object, Obi's fiancée. It is possible that Achebe points to Clara's diminution as an example of how society determines people's behavior and attitude. Since women's positions tend to be somehow subordinate in Obi's Nigerian society, on her return home, the narrator describes Clara as conforming to traditional women's roles. With her return to Lagos, she is expected to marry for the reason that as Philomena Okeke argues "when women do not marry, regardless of their beauty or social skills, the Igbo suspect something is either wrong with the single woman herself or with her social background. They identify her as immoral, stigmatized, or simply unlucky" (241).

Achebe suggests that Clara would have been an ideal partner for Obi as she devotes herself completely to their relationship and is the only one who assists him financially and selflessly. For example when Obi is in dire need of money, she helps him by giving him fifty pounds. Initially, Obi is baffled about how Clara had saved such a large amount of money, but the narrative states that she "was reasonably well paid and she had not studied nursing on any progressive union's scholarship" (NLAE 107). Being a woman and also an Osu, Clara may not have enjoyed the privilege of a scholarship from the Umuofia union, an organization that is part of the system that eventually works to oppress Obi. Clara is made somewhat exempt from this oppression precisely because she is an outsider and a woman. And yet, this oppression may also have made her free. And though Obi is aware that Umuofia has been conditioned to repel outcasts, had he gone ahead with his marriage, he would have set a good example of fighting segregation as he had wanted to do on the issue of fighting corruption.

Certainly Igbo society is conditioned on the caste system. The beliefs of the people are seen to be deeply rooted in their culture and colonization has not altered it completely. Apart from the fact that Clara and Obi are prevented from marrying based on the caste system, marriage is perceived as much more than a union between a man and woman. In their book Two Voices from Nigeria: Nigeria through the Literature of Chinua Achebe and Buchi Emecheta, Lyn Reese and Rick Clarke explain that marriage

> was a contract between two extended families and was arranged, tying two descent groups economically and socially. The contract was sealed through the payment of a bride price. This was not payment for a wife but rather payment which strengthened the alliance between the two families.... Romantic, individual choice love was not felt to be the basis for a good match. (16)

Although Obi's choice of a wife is based on romantic love, he still must seek the consent of his parents who are more concerned about their own social acceptance in society than about his happiness. Some parents specifically choose their children's partners but in situations where they do not, parents most often expect their children to marry from decent families and bring honor to their names. Toyin Falola sheds more light on this issue of marriage in Culture and Customs of Nigeria:

> While arranged marriages have declined in importance, men and women still announce their choices and decisions to their parents and other family members with the hope that consent will be granted. Parents ask questions regarding ethnicity, town of origin, religion, and occupation to ensure that a good choice has been made. Most parents still prefer that their children marry a member of the same ethnic group as themselves. (120)

Igbo parents believe they should have a say in who their children marry. They may not impose brides or grooms on their children as they did in the past, but they express their concerns when their children decide to marry from families of which they do not approve, just as Obi's parents do in his case. As such, family background plays a key role in determining whether parents would give their consent to a prospective marriage or not.

Faced with such complexities, it could be said that in trying to solve their problems, Clara is more rational. When she initially suggests they part ways, Obi can only think, even if jokingly, that it is because he borrowed money from her. He informs her, "You don't want to marry someone who has to borrow money to pay for his insurance. He knew it was a grossly unfair and false accusation, but wanted her to be on the defensive" (NLAE 124). Obi irrationally puts Clara on the "defensive" because he believes it will be a blow to his manhood if Clara is the one who provides for him rather than vice versa. By contrast, her final step in deciding not to see him again, even though she is pregnant, reveals her as a sensible person who knows he is not man enough for her. Obi's decision that Clara should give him time to allow things to cool off exposes him as one who wants time to meet the impossible demands of both family and lover. Unable to choose, he remains weak, impotent, living in a world of fantasy. Obi fails to come to terms with the fact that it is not just his society that is still prejudiced, but he also is.

Sadly the existing structures make it impossible for Clara to solemnize her relationship in marriage. Because the society is immersed in schism, and because she realizes that Obi has been emasculated, she painfully relinquishes the relationship she has labored for and which she hopes would end in a union. For a woman who has devoted much of her time, love, and life to Obi, Clara seems to be more on the receiving end because apart from her gender as a woman, she also bears the stigma of an Osu which might make it much more difficult for her to start a new relationship, assuming she would even attempt one. Breaking an association which has involved such commitment is obviously not an easy decision for her to make. At various times we do observe she attempts to end their relationship which Obi seems to think is unwarranted. So we can understand her comments when she painfully says to Obi "You are making things difficult for yourself. How many times did I tell you that we were deceiving ourselves? ...Anyway, it doesn't matter. There is no need for long talk" (NLAE 143). As a result, we find Clara's pain to be reflected in her statement when she admits: "There is only one thing I regret. I should have known better" (NLAE 142), and "I ought to have been able to take care of myself" (NLAE 143). By extrapolation she is angry at herself for getting pregnant for Obi. To an extent we sympathize with her since she is the one who would possibly bear the shame of their act and trauma of going through an abortion. So we observe that Clara is deprived of a life with Obi, and as Palmer points out, Achebe "wishes to show that Obi's love affair with Clara is destroyed by his society's conservatism" (70). But the issue is does Achebe see her as having any possibility? Any hope? Or is it a hope only to be found because she has finally turned her back on Obi, who is no longer her "home"? Although the society might still be reserved, there is hope for Clara not just because she has left Obi, but because changes happen in societies, and Igbo society is not excluded from this.

On the basis of the foregoing, one finds the exit of Hannah and Clara from Obi's life particularly significant because this is where lies the tragedy of these women's lives and the raging conflict in Obi towards both. His reaction and feeling to their departure as we see is a combination of relief and sadness. On one hand Hannah's death is a reprieve to Obi as he could guiltily remember "her as the woman who got things done" (NLAE 165). Although he does mourn her loss, his remembrance of her in this way probably suggests that Obi might perhaps have perceived his mother as someone who had exerted too much dominance in his life. For a man who just lost a loved one, his ability to sleep soundly and his healthy appetite suggest a psychological state of depressurization. Moreover as Obi muses, "I wonder why I am feeling like a brand-new snake just emerged from its slough" (NLAE 165), as he suppresses the hard-working memory of his mother.

On the other hand, Achebe highlights Clara's exodus as a painful loss to Obi –one that shows his frailty and dependence on her. Though Clara might be seen as a loving and compassionate partner to Obi -one who, after he decided to separate from her, caused him "many anxious days and sleepless nights that he had passed through" (NLAE 156),Obi still sees her as a threat to him. Rather than be grateful that she helps with his loan, for example, he is worried about his ego, how such a loan reflects upon him. This dependence reveals him as a weak man who cannot make decisions on his own. This ambivalence is emphasized when he contacts a doctor to perform an abortion for Clara. We see that Obi briefly contemplates returning to Clara and going ahead with his plans to marry her. As the narrative goes, after dropping Clara at the doctor's office and seeing her leave with the doctor, "Obi wanted to rush out of his car and shout: 'Stop. Let's go and get married now,' but he couldn't and didn't" (NLAE 149). He gives up the chance to display that he is a man, capable of taking charge of his own affairs and starting life with Clara. The hope for a future generation dies with the abortion of Clara's pregnancy.

By contrast to Achebe's bleak assessment of his characters' future, Nigeria's future, in No Longer at Ease, in Anthills of the Savannah, Achebe's characters – especially women– find success through the spirit of reconciliation in Anthills of the Savannah. Through his female characters, Beatrice, Agatha, and Elewa, Achebe underscores the importance of putting aside our differences and deciding what role we want to play in society. These female characters as we see are of different classes and backgrounds, yet they are able to find solace in one another's support despite the political upheaval that claims the lives of the three disputing friends –Sam, the President of Kangan; Chris, Commissioner for Information and Beatrice's fiancé; and Ikem, the Newspaper Editor and Elewa's Fiancé. These women's disagreements between demonstrate that humans do have divergent perspectives that must be overcome, but in reconciling their differences, they can possess their own destinies.

It is Beatrice, an epitome of the modern woman, depicted as goddess and daughter of Idemili, who needs to define a place for herself in society, regardless of social structures that still tend to be discriminatory towards women. In "The Black Woman and the Problem of Gender: An African Perspective", Ali Mazrui examines sexism from different angles: benevolent, benign, and malignant. He defines benevolent sexism "as a form of discrimination which is protective or generous towards the otherwise underprivileged gender" (211), benign as a sexism that "acknowledges gender differences without bestowing sexual advantage or inflicting a gender cost" (214), and malignant as the "most pervasive and most insidious" because it "subjects women to economic manipulation, sexual exploitation and political marginalization" (218). These categories, especially the benign and malignant, are reflected in both Achebe's works. For instance, it is in reaction to the derogatory role that Beatrice believes Sam places her that she refuses to accept and function in the role he assigned to her as a guide to the American journalist. At first, Beatrice thinks she is invited to the party to reconcile Sam with Chris and Ikem, but in realizing what he wanted her to do, especially when she perceives that the journalist has the attention of all the men, she becomes defiant by becoming snobbish to the journalist and refusing to play the role of guide. Obviously using her sexuality to lure Sam away is not the proper approach to protest her perceived injustice and prove a point since she is reverting to the same sexuality she claims should not be used against her by behaving in an improper manner. Beatrice feels she has been misinterpreted as a person, and this misunderstanding may be due to the way people perceive her personality. As she says,

[t]here is one account of me it seems I will never get used to, which can still bring tears into my eyes. Ambitious. Me ambitious! How? And it is this truly unjust presentation that's forcing me to expose my life on these pages to see if perhaps there are aspects of me I had successfully concealed even from myself. (AS 77)

For Beatrice to make this statement shows that she is willing to examine herself to determine if she has her own faults in order to recast her steps and correct her attitude towards others. Hyden notes that individuals often possess a combination of (vertical and horizontal) cleavages; "persons characterized by such crosscutting cleavages are more tolerant of others because they can more easily empathize with people coming from perspectives different from their own" (191). But that is not the case with Beatrice initially since she is not tolerant towards Agatha. In her relations with Agatha, for example, there is a class difference: their employer/employee relationship had remained strictly frosty. Beatrice claims:

I made it clear to her from the start that I wasn't ready yet to wash and wipe the feet of my paid help. It is quite enough that I have to do the weekly grocery at the Gelegele market while she is clapping her hands and rolling her eyes and hips at some hairy-chested prophet in white robes and shower caps. (AS 760)

Their association shows that Beatrice fails to understand or respect Agatha's religious beliefs and does not attempt to make any compromise. But a fascinating twist to the novel is what is depicted in Agatha's case, that is, her antagonism toward Elewa who stays with Beatrice after the demise of Ikem. Agatha's reaction is also surprising. It is in reaction to their class structure that Agatha feels she is justified in serving Elewa a meal that befits someone of her social class. Beatrice's thoughts give us a glimpse of Agatha's character:

After the first surge of anger Beatrice found herself feeling for the first time for this poor, desiccated, sanctimonious girl something she had never before thought of extending to her – pity. Yes, she thought, her Agatha deserved to be pitied; this girl who danced and raved about salvation from dawn to dusk every Saturday, who distributed free leaflets (she had once even sneaked up to Chris when Beatrice stepped out of the room and given him one). Yes, this Agatha who was so free with leaflets dripping with the saving blood of Jesus and yet had no single drop of charity in her own anaemic blood. (AS 168)

Someone who devotes most of her time attending church services and preaching the gospel might be expected to show the tenets of her belief, that is, to show love and kindness. Yet the hypocritical Agatha maltreats Elewa, a woman who just lost a loved one and who is in need of love and compassion. So we do understand when Beatrice berates and calls her "a very stupid girl and a very wicked person" (AS 167). She is "stupid" in the sense that she is contradicting herself by failing to reach out to Elewa and indeed deserves "pity" because she fails to bond with Elewa. Despite these discrepancies in class and perception, Achebe insinuates that even in the midst of chaos, differences, and oppression, women can still find a common ground, a link to bind them. And it is at this juncture that Elewa's character comes in to play. She brings about the spirit of reconciliation, effected through the sudden death of her fiancé, Ikem, and in the birth of her baby girl, Amaechina, whose name is a masculine one that means "May-the-path-never-close" (AS 206). Elewa is a sales girl, who lives in the ghetto with her mother, a fish seller. But she is Ikem's girlfriend; a man –

the editor of the reputable newspaper, National Gazette, to be precise – who overlooks the bridge of the social division to date a girl of Elewa's class. Through Elewa's relationship with Ikem, she is able to develop and maintain a relationship with Beatrice. So we see the class difference between these two women: Elewa, a woman who did not complete her education and cannot speak Standard English, and Beatrice, a woman who has a first-class degree from a foreign university, overcome through their mutual respect for Ikem. It is important to note that it is through Ikem that the question of what women want is posed. Ikem's status as a writer and political activist gives him the opportunity to advocate for the masses. But even in his role as advocate, he excludes women as we discover in Beatrice's accusation that he has no role for the womenfolk in his political agenda. Ikem sees women as useful only as a last resort for solving problems. According to Beatrice,

In the last couple of years we have argued a lot about what I have called the chink in his armory of brilliant and original ideas. I tell him he has no clear role for women in his political thinking; and he doesn't seem to be able to understand it. Or didn't until near the end. (AS 83)

Of course Ikem does acknowledge the truth of this accusation when he says, "Your charge has forced me to sit down and contemplate the nature of oppression – how flexible it must learn to be, how many faces it must learn to wear if it is to succeed again and again" (AS 88-89). In this comment, Ikem surely serves as the voice of Achebe, and yet he insists it is the womenfolk who need to define the role they want to play in society. We see that Beatrice takes the initiative by pointing out to Ikem what his perception of women has been. Without her showing his lapse, Ikem would not have realized his error in his thinking toward women.

Moreover Achebe seems to be suggesting that regardless of class or social status, be it political, economic, or social, women need to be united in fighting patriarchy, united in carrying out our common goals. As hooks also points out, "There can be no mass-based feminist movement to end sexist oppression without a unified front – women must take the initiative and demonstrate the power of solidarity"(396-397). hooks means that there will be no modification to what we want if there is no unified front on our part. Ultimately it is because we need to act on a collective basis that we see Achebe's female characters united at the end of the novel. Because of the bonding between Beatrice and Elewa, regardless of their class, they are able to comfort each other after the demise of their men. Moreover it is because of this bond between them that Beatrice is able to perform the naming ceremony of Elewa's daughter, an event that should have been carried out by a male, Elewa's uncle. If there was no agreement on the part of Elewa to that effect, Beatrice would not have been able to conduct the ceremony. These women settled their differences within and among themselves. As we see, Beatrice takes the step to apologize to and comfort Agatha, an action she has never done before whenever she castigates Agatha. Elewa does not bear any grudge against Agatha for the inhumane way she treats her and Agatha shows her happiness by dancing herself off and leading the praise worship during the naming ceremony of Elewa's daughter.

Again if we are to go by Mazrui's explanation of benign sexism and apply it to the depiction of Beatrice giving the child a male name, could that be considered as benign sexism because Mazrui contends that "the distinction between feminine names and masculine names is still fundamentally a case of benign sexism" (215). Although gender names might seem sexist, in this case the moniker is a significant one that hopes for continued women liberation and empowerment. This depiction might be an attempt to strike a balance in gender. Because it is Beatrice rather than her uncle who carries out this function, implicitly we are given the impression that women are equally capable of playing leadership roles in the social and political affairs of their societies.

And so we are left to ask ourselves what Achebe says about women. What societal role does he ascribe to them? Achebe suggests that women are strong, reliable, and competent, and to envisage an equal place in society for women through these fictional characters. He is careful, however, not to impose his view of what this role should be. Indeed without any initiative from women, it will be difficult to pursue our goals. The end results of these women's lives are very much different. Although Hannah and Clara seem to have something in common in their love for Obi, there is no means for them to reach a compromise socially because their society is embroiled in conflict. Consequently their inability to reconcile societal barriers results in the tragedy of these lives. However we see the other women: Beatrice, Agatha, and Elewa find something to connect them together – their strength to resolve their differences and forge a common front despite the political calamity that consumes their loved ones. This solidarity is the feature Achebe captures and brings to the fore of this novel to show the love and compassion these women are able to develop towards one another.

Chapter 8

Female Sexuality in Bessora's Novel

JW Bouchard

IN Deux bébés et l'addition, mainstream definitions of gender and sexuality are represented as reliant on specific categorizations based on Cartesian "taxonomies" that revealed themselves most prominently in nineteenth century studies of gender and sexuality. As race, feminist and gender theories continue to move from general to more localized views of identitarian issues, we bear witness to literary voices who present non-essentialized protagonists emerging from a specific set of cultural and individual factors. French immigrant authors such as Bessora participate in a chorus of "queer" or "abnormal" voices that Spanish theorist Beatriz Preciado calls "les multitudes." Preciado's discussion of "les multitudes" focuses primarily on physical "difference" and the discourses surrounding intersex or transsexual subjectivities within the Western European context. However, her theory could also be applied to figures who retain an "intersex" identity by resisting normative masculine codes of behavior. In both cases, the "abnormal one" disturbs the foundational French ideals of fixed gender identity that have been perpetuated through centuries of universalist discourse. Within this framework, the cultural significance of Yéno, the protagonist and narrator of Bessora's Deux bébés et l'addition can be analyzed.

Yéno is indeed transgressive, in that he both counters and challenges Western discourses on gender, employment, sexuality, and health. In Deux bébés et l'addition, mainstream definitions of race, gender and sexuality are represented as reliant on specific categorizations, or Cartesian "taxonomies," that revealed themselves most prominently in seventeenth century French colonial projects and nineteenth century studies of gender and sexuality.

A highly political author, all five of Bessora's novels seek to subvert French definitions of race, gender, and sexuality in the immigrant context. An immigrant herself (of Gabonese and Swiss descent), Bessora's literary projects fuse autobiographical content and fictionalized representations of current political realities facing France's immigrant populations. Within this framework, Bessora offers the reader protagonists who simultaneously serve as models of "abnormality" or "difference," and surpass the limiting identitarian categories imposed upon them. Along with racial "difference," Bessora is particularly concerned with issues surrounding gender identity. In a 2002 article on gender, Bessora writes: "Le biologique n'implique pas un rôle social…il n'y existe pas de fait masculine ou feminine, mais des représentations qui se négocient sans cesse." ("La question du genre" 1). To underscore this notion, Bessora gives us protagonists such as Yéno, who goes against all "rôle sociaux" assigned to his gender and is constantly negotiating his unique identity amidst scathing social discourses regarding normative constructions of gender, sexuality, and acceptable forms of employment in the French nation. His identity is particularly problematic in the eyes of the nation because of his ambiguous sexuality and feminized persona.

In France, mainstream conceptions of gender and sexuality are still informed by specific categorizations that revealed themselves most prominently in nineteenth century Western studies of sexology. Firmly rooted in the biomedical field, studies such as those produced by the research of Havelock Ellis and Richard Freiherr Krafft-Ebing were inextricably linked to discussions of health and the "normal body," While both scholars relied on the binary categories of normalcy and inversion, the nuances of their arguments differed greatly. An important difference between Krafft-Ebing and Ellis is they way in which each categorized "inversion" or homosexuality and other "abnormal" sexual behaviors as pathogological (Krafft-Ebing) or as suppressed desires that are part of normal human sexuality (Ellis). Krafft-Ebing defined these behaviors as paresthesia or "perversion of the sexual instinct" due to misplaced desire onto objects, body parts other than the primary sexual organs, or members of the same sex. However, Ellis's work is well known for its sympathy toward individuals who were attracted to members of the same sex, a certain body part, or an inanimate fetish object, all qualities that apply to Yéno and will be discussed in subsequent portions of this study. He was a pioneering advocate for the right of "inverts" of both sexes to experience erotic pleasure and social acceptance. Whereas Ellis sought to demystify these "normal" behaviors, Krafft-Ebing asserted that these "deviant" sexual practices (such as homosexuality and "cross-dressing") were curable.

Particularly relevant to the French context is this notion that the "sexually deviant" category of homosexuality was viewed as "degenerative," or a regression to a "primitive state." Such selective terminology hacks back to seventeenth-century discourses on the colonized "Other," who was, in the eyes of the French, a savage in need of both spiritual redemption and cultural education. Given France's problematic colonial history, this notion takes on a noteworthy significance in twentieth and twentieth-century discussions of immigration. The homosexual (or "sexually deviant") immigrant is not only doubly "othered" as a result of both race and sexuality, but he is also viewed as a "degenerate" and transgressive element that endangers the health of the French republican nation. In The Frail Social Body, Carolyn Dean reveals the importance of "bodily integrity" to the definition of French citizenship. As her study reveals, in interwar France, homosexuality was thought of as so powerful that it could infect or even undo the French "social body." Referring to present day French politics, Preciado expands on this notion of infection or infiltration in a spatial framework:

Le corps de la multitude queer apparaît au centre de ce que j'appellerai, pour reprendre une expression de Deleuze et Guattari, un travail de "déterritorialisation" de l'hétéroseuxalité. Une déterritorialisation qui affecte aussi bien l'espace urbain (il faut donc parler de déterritorialisation de l'espace majoritaire et non de ghetto) que l'espace corporel. (20)

To combat this spatial or "corporal" infiltration of the "Other," France has turned to universalizing discourses, which have historically served as a sort of vaccination for the national body. Thus, French universalism is premised on idea that anyone can become French, so long as they are willing to subscribe to the specific philosophies and ideologies that make up the French nation. Since this time, universalism has been taken to be the defining trait of the French Republic and its most enduring value. It also shapes current political realities and policies on immigration. Until an immigrant is assimilated into the French universal definition of citizenship, he or she is the ultimate "Other." In an article tracing the evolution of French universalist thought, Naomi Schorr writes: "Achieving French identity requires as the wages of assimilation the renunciation of public cultural particularism in the name of France's vaunted particularity, its "singularity," in short, its universalism." (50). As far as identity is concerned, the universal or "default" French identity is, of course, heterosexual and White. As Beatriz Preciado rightly indicates, in France and elsewhere, heterosexuality is not simply the norm, but also an imposed political regime in the Foucauldian sense.

En travaillant dans une perspective déjà explorée par Audre Lorde, Ti-Grace Atkinson, et le manifeste "The Woman-Identified-Woman" des "Radicalesbians", Wittig en était arrivee à décrire l'hétérosexualité non pas comme une pratique sexuelle mais comme un régime politique, comme faisant partie de l'administration des corps et de la gestion calculée de la vie, et relevant de la "biopolitique". Une lecture croisée de Wittig et de Foucault aurait permis dès le début des années 80 de donner une definition de l'hétérosexualité comme technologie bio-politique destinée à produire des corps straight. ("Multitudes queer" 18)

The identitarian requirements imposed by French Universalism have historically supported the form of heterosexual politics described by Preciado. Furthermore, such requirements are racially exclusive. As a result of these stringent, "universal" guidelines (which, in their most extreme form require a denial of the self and all previous cultural affiliations), miscegenation, hybridity and multiculturalism (all contained in the French term métissage) have been at the center of many debates and continue to raise questions on the social, political, cultural, artistic and literary scenes. Many postmodern scholars agree on the erroneous nature of the term miscegenation, (based on the axiom presupposing the existence of different races within the human species that was born out of modern taxonomical practice), however one must to recognize miscegenation as a concrete cultural and social phenomenon as well as a very real way to define a category of individuals according today's French society.

Though Bessora's Yéno is forced into this limited (and limiting) category by French society, he resists such categorizations thanks to his corporal, historical, and psychological individualities and his racial and cultural métissage. In Deux bébés et l'addition, Yéno not only transgresses these universal codes, but also undoes them, exemplifying the need for the French nation to recognize its changing population and the need to reorganize the fixed structures that determine "normalcy" and "alterity" within this context. An entire study could be done on Yéno's racial and cultural métissage as a signifier of difference. Though I will not be able to cover in detail the identitarian and transgressive themes associated with hybridity and race within this particular project, suffice it to say that Yéno's particular form of gender/sexual transgression is intensely heightened by the fact he is the son of a Black, African mother and a White, French father (conceived in a former French colony). In addition to his race, Yéno's performance of his masculinity/femininity - through his choice of career, his ambivalent sexuality, and his troubled relationship with his mother (that results in both physical and psychological illness) – are both transgressive and productive in the French context.

Yéno is the postmodern hero par excellence, and defies all definitions of "normalcy" imposed on him by French republican values. His identity is fragmented, unresolved, and ambiguous. He does not act, and rather allows himself to be acted upon by his sister, Waura, her husband, Modeste, and his love interest, Nidale. In the sections to follow, I will detail the ways in which Yéno transgresses normative definitions of gender, sexuality, and health before moving into a discussion of the productive possibilities associated with the identitarian model he represents.

Performing Gender: The sage-femme

If "gender is an act which has been rehearsed, much as a script survives the particular actors who make use of it, but which requires individual actors in order to be actualized and reproduced as reality once again," (Butler 526) then Yéno is so far off the script that no social "prompt" of gender normalcy could hope to remind him of the "correct" line. Yéno works as a sage-femme (midwife) in the novel. In French, as in English, there is no specifically masculine term for a "male midwife." This semantic restriction, indicative of the highly gendered nature of the profession, prohibits Yéno from being truly "masculine" in the eyes of the French. Throughout he novel, Yéno is asked by both French and immigrant mothers who come into the hospital why he didn't become a gynecologist, which would have been a more acceptable form of employment for a man. He is considered to be a professional failure, opting for an inferior, feminine position. The reason for Yéno's professional "failure" is ostensibly a lack of motivation, or his willingness to remain in a passive (feminine) role. Yéno's passivity is exemplified early on in his existence when compared to his twin sister, Waura, who was apparently the most "masculine" of the embryos to inhabit the mother's womb.

At the beginning of the novel, the reader learns that Yéno's twin sister, Waura, ate the triplet who at one time shared the uterus with them. Waura preyed on this feminized embryo who "déjà à l'état d'embryon, ne supportait aucune concurrence et souffrait d'un grave délire paranoïaque" (54). Waura's act is essentially a

Darwinian gesture. To assure her survival and acceptance by her mother, Waura consumes the weaker element, simultaneously providing her with extra nourishment and doing away with a potential competitor for her mother's love and affection. Though Yéno is present during this event, he does nothing to stop his sister from consuming the weaker element, nor does he consume it himself. The dynamics of Waura and Yéno's relationship are established at this point, and Waura's tendency to dominate Yéno persists throughout the novel. Thus, Yéno is doubly-feminized: first, as a result of passive relationship with his sister, and second, because of his career choice.

Yéno's choice to become a mid-wife was a highly personal one, informed by his problematic past with his mother. As he explains, his job is a form of therapy.

"J'accouche les femmes qui on du plomb dans le ventre. Quand une femme enfante avec moi, j'ai l'illusion de rejouer mon passé; la tête du bébé paraît, et je me vois au même âge: ma nassiance de déroule sous mes yeux…L'enfantement est pour moi une sorte de rite qui me ramène à mes origins, sauf que je voudrais changer l'histoire." (Bessora7)

On a political level, by choosing to be a sage-femme, Yéno performs a "dés-identification" that supports the notion of "les multitudes queer":

"Dés-identifications," (pour reprendre la formulation de De Lauretis), identifications stratégiques, détournement des technologies du corps et désontologisations du sujet de la politique sexuelle, telles sont quelques unes des strategies politiques des multitudes queer." (Preciado 21)

He takes the role of sage-femme out of a strictly feminine space and appropriates it as a way in which to sort out his complicated past.

Rehearsing Sexuality: Yéno vs. Modeste

Yéno's difference is further emphasized by his brother-in-law (ironically named Modeste). Modeste, a successful gynecologist, serves as a powerful, hyper-masculine foil to Yéno's feminized, asexual persona. Modeste is quick to indicate that, as a doctor, he is capable of curing and is thus productive in society. He continually proves his "productivity" but serially impregnating the mid-wifery and nursing staff at his and Yéno's place of employment. Yéno, a midwife, can only assist in delivering babies and make the mothers' experiences more comfortable. Thus, he is a feminine caregiver, the opposite of Modeste's "puissant," masculine force.

Aside from their social/professional personas, the main sexual difference between Modeste and Yéno is the way in which each "rehearses" his sexuality. By impregnating Waura and others, Modeste proves his virility time after time. If, like gender, sexuality is something that must be performed, then Modeste's promiscuity is a way of assuring his straight identity. Yéno, however, never engages in sexual acts in the novel. In fact, he rarely discusses his physical attraction to men or women, unless he is fetishizing Nidale's ears (to be discussed further). As Bernard De Meyer writes:

> Son identité sexuelle est également ambivalente: alors qu'il est clairement un homme qui aime les femmes (il est vrain, d'un amour platonique le plus souvent), il montre des tendances homo-érotiques…il a quelque chose de subversif, à la fois en lui-même et dans ses nombreuses metamorphoses; aussi change-t-il pour un oui ou un non, comme son prénom (à l'anglaise) pourait le suggérer. (21)

As De Meyer indicates, Yéno's constantly shifting sexuality, which is never rehearsed and thus never classifiable, renders him a subversive element in a Cartesian society that privileges clarity and organization. Yéno's ambivalent bisexuality is decidedly postmodern, according to Ken Plummer's study on stories of sexuality. He states that unlike their linear and unified modernist counterparts, postmodern sexual stories are full of indeterminacies, multiple possibilities, and changing or blurring identities. It is this second category that best applies to Yéno. In his transgression lies the possibility to overcome negative stereotypes that have been imposed on him and to move beyond binary constructions of gender and sexuality toward a more fragmented, liberated sense of self.

Normative Health and Fragmented Relations

Not only is Yéno's identity fragmented and ambiguous, his mother's is as well. Throughout the novel, he maintains a conversation with "Utérus chéri," a corporally, temporally, and spatially fragmented representation of his mother who left him and Waura at birth. His conversations with this fragmented entity are the only ways in which he is able to come to terms with his own anger and sense of abandonment. Throughout the novel, he poses series of questions to Utérus that are never answered, thus augmenting his sense of separation from her and from any "normal" model of a parent-child relationship. Yéno's communication with Utérus is rendered even more problematic as a result of his polarized emotional stance. Utérus is at once loved and hated, sought after and scolded:

"Vous nous avez pondu comme on commande le café: 'deux bébés et l'addition. Même pas s'il vous plaît. Ni merci. Ni au revoir. L'addition, je la paye encore. Et avec le pourboire,' reproche-t-il à l'Utérus aimé et haï à la fois" (Bessora 32)

In Gender Trouble, Butler critics they ways in which Freudian "grand narratives" privilege certain stories or patterns of identifications that supposedly produce a unified gendered self. As Freud claims, the primary element necessary for forming a (gendered) self is the relationship one has with one's mother and father (the secondary relationship would be that with one's siblings). Butler contests this idea, and develops the notion that gendered subjectivity is instead a "history of identifications, parts of which can be brought into play in given contexts and which, precisely because they encode the contingencies of personal history, do not always point back to an internal coherence of any kind." (Butler 331).

This applies directly to Yéno, considering the fact his mother left him at birth and played a minor role in his "gendered" development. His interactions with his sister and Modeste greatly inform his conceptions of gender and, in turn, his internal "conversations" with his fragmented mother.

His mother's abandonment engendered a series of "illnesses" or "paranoia" in Yéno, adding further to his feminized persona. In Western medical terms, the "conversations" Yéno holds with his mother would be diagnosed as mental illness. In addition, Yéno blames his inner-ear condition on his mother's absence. His sense of separation from society and exclusion from all "normal" categories of male identity is heightened by a birth defect resulting in his "acouphène mélancholique," a continual static in his right ear that transforms normal words into incomprehensible sonic transmissions resembling surrealist sound poetry.

The only temporary cure he has found to deal with the symptoms of his condition is to constantly eat raw carrots. This necessitates his leaving crucial situations both at work and in his personal life to attend to his auditory maladies. As a result, he is unable to engage in a "healthy" romantic relationship with Nidale or anyone else for that matter. In addition, because of his own hearing problems, Yéno becomes obsessed with babies' ears as well as Nidale's. He develops what would be termed as "unhealthy" obsessions and fetishes that distract him in his work, during his time with Nidale and with his political group, "La ligue des sage-femmes révolutionnaires." However, he can never be fully cured of his ear problem, since it is what permits him to achieve the desired unification with Utérus. It serves as a translator, connecting Yéno with his disembodied mother and simultaneously separating him from the rest of society.

Yéno and "les multitudes"

As a result of these myriad "abnormalities," Yéno is unclassifiable according to the limiting categories for gender, sexuality, and health imposed by the French nation. He is the ultimate "Other," an outsider, a marginalized figure. However, to leave a reading of Deux bébés et l'addition at this simplistic conclusion would be to deny the work of its social relevance and transformative power. Reading Bessora's novel in conjunction with Preciado's theory "les multitudes queer," one realizes that Yéno is a literary example of Preciado's "abnormal ones." Yéno's character is the result of myriad lived experiences and associations that have shaped his gender and sexuality. Returning to Butler, Yéno's particular performance of his gender does not rely on his identification with one sex or one object (i.e. his mother, Waura, Modeste). Rather, his gender is composed of a set of internalized signs, imposed on his psychic sense of identity. Therefore, his gender identity is fragmented, mutable, and constantly subject to further exterior influence.

In many ways, Preciado picks up where Butler left off. Taking the notion that "in [gender's] very character as performative resides the possibility of contesting its reified status." (Butler "Performative Acts" 520), Preciado theorizes ways in which "the multitudes" are capable of undoing fixed categories of gender and sexual performance. As she makes clear in her Manifeste contra-sexuel, Preciado bases her work on the notion that sexuality is something we "put on," in the postmodern sense, something that can be traded, commodified, and altered. In this way, she undoes the very categories that create marginalized subjects and restores power to those who cannot be contained by received definitions of gender and sexuality.

Preciado states that multiplicity is not "Otherness," since the latter would imply simply going against a hegemonic norm (and thus still adhering to these fixed systems of definition). Instead, "les multitudes" aim to proliferate the notion that in order to completely subvert the traditional institutions (which aim to be sovereign and universal), one must necessarily oppose the sexopolitical, straight epistemologies that still dominate scientific discourses on sexuality. As Preciado states, the multitudes are not simply transgressive, since this would imply alterity and marginality. Their goal is to reorganize these systems of knowledge (and the cultural definitions they produce) in order to undo the binaries between states of normalcy and alterity, thus doing away with the phenomenon of marginality all together. Yéno is representative of a member of "les multitudes" since he not only surpasses dominant systems of categorization (through his career, sexuality, and health), but also disrupts the notion of fixed gender identity that produces these categories. Such literary representations of "les multitudes" are significant on a very quotidian level in that they bring "abnormal" characters like Yéno into public focus, presenting them not as "queer," but as individuals attempting to come to terms with their own psychological problems and familial situations.

Through Yéno, Bessora appropriates the systems of knowledge that create "difference" and subsequently subverts them to call into question what constitutes "normalcy" and "deviancy" in terms of race, sexuality and gender specifically within the French context of immigration. Through the creation of protagonists such as Yéno, Bessora joins the "French" multiplicity of voices that protest against normative identitarian constructs and beyond that, open up new discursive terrains for identity articulation through literary representation.

Chapter 9

Enekwe's Feminine Archetypes

C Schneider

BARBARA Melosh in her book Gender and American History Since 1890 posits that "gender" is socially constructed. Her classic example comes from Nineteenth-century Victorian culture which she notes,

> described sexual difference in terms of the duties and obligations that followed from men's and women's inherent characteristics. Women's moral superiority made them ideal wives and mothers, charged with the solemn responsibility of guiding errant children and men. ("Introduction" 7)

Many socially constructed notions have been perpetuated through the literary works and philosophies of many societies. Elaine Showalter in her paper "Towards a Feminist Poetics" is of the opinion that when we study "stereotypes of women, the sexism of male critics", and the "limited roles" women play in literary history, "we are not learning what women have felt and experienced, but what men have thought women should be" (34-36). Hence recent Feminist interest in literary criticism is directed at exposing how ideas of gender and gender relationships are constructed and transmitted through literary works. This paper assesses how Onuora Enekwe's portrayal of women pander to archetypal inscriptions of women as either mother (the Madonna) or destroyer (la femme fatale) – masculinist portraitures which aid in entrenching contestable notions and myths of male superiority and female inferiority. In contesting phallocentric systems of thought and dismantling logocentricism, Feminist criticism challenges Masculinist female (mis)perceptions and (mis)presentations while simultaneously deconstructing patriarchal "systems of thought which legitimize themselves by reference to some presence or point of authority prior to and outside of themselves" (Hawthorn 130).

The image and personality of women in Enekwe's oeuvres easily come across with a critical view of some poems in Enekwe's three collections – Broken Pots (published in 1977), Marching to Kilimanjaro (published in 2005) and Gentle Birds Come to me (published in 2007). These supposedly evidence the poet's concern for women and their well being. However the poet perceives and subsequently inscribes women as what Selden and Widdowson term "beings of subjectivity" (189). Throughout Enekwe's poetry, two major archetypes are purveyed of women: Women as destroyers, the femme fatale, and women as mothers, the madonna-child. In much of poetry as in other genres, literary archetypes, being "recurrent narrative designs, patterns of action, character types or images identifiable in a wide variety of works of literature as well as myths", are usually held to reflect "a set of universal, primitive and elemental mental forms or patterns whose effective embodiment in a literary work evokes a profound response from the reader" (Abrams 224). In thus appraising and challenging some feminine archetypes in Enekwe's poetry it will be seen that readers may have been misled into holding erroneous conjectures that subtly impact upon their assessment of womanhood. Instances of such misplacement are obvious from Enekwe's deliberate contortions which serve to undermine femaleness and perpetuate the stereotype of her as a being of simple qualities. No doubt both ideas are borne out of male phallocentric and masculinist attempts to culturally dominate and relegate women to subservient positions the world over.

The Femme Fatale

In discussing archetypal femme fatale images constructed in Enekwe's poetry, we turn to the poems "Lady Death" (Broken Pots) and "Prayer for Peace" (Marching to Kilimamjaro) as examples. Although both poems are published in different anthologies by Enekwe – in fact, the latter is published twenty eight years after the former – yet we see the poet exploring the same notion of women in both poems.

In "Lady Death" the destructive woman of Shaw's imagining is reflected through the image of a female praying mantis whose actions are reported by the male "voice". It begins with a sarcastic comment on the idea of love between man and woman: "Love can be a dangerous game" he observes. Where or how this danger originates is not clear. The next line never takes us to any raison'd'etre for this overture between man and woman in love (referred to here as "Mantis" and "his lady"). By refusing to provide some explanatory details which the signposts of "love game" suggests, the poet insults our intelligence. However, what follows is even more disturbing as the poetic voice describes a macabre "love" and "death" dance:

> in the region of terrible heat
> she clasps him within her thighs
> ensconces his head between her teeth
> and with the swiftness of guillotine blade
> chops it off... (Pots 30)

Now we are provided the persona's own simplistic, if not prosaic, explanation for the murderous instinct of the female species:

> so the dance can endure
> without remorse or wasteful introspection. (30)

No doubt this succeeds more in establishing the wickedness of the perpetrator of the action rather than explicating the situations that give rise to it. By this Enekwe condemns the woman for heinous crimes and sentences her to states of criminality, irrationality and stupidity. It is similar to Jane Tompkins's observations in the movie Gunfight at the OK Corral where two characters Doc Halliday and Jo Van Fleet star as degraded characters. Tompkins remarks that

Doc Holliday is a similarly degraded character. He used to be a dentist and is now a gambler, who lives to get other people's money away from them; he is a drunk, and he abuses the woman that loves him. But his weaknesses, in the perspective of the movie, are glamorous. He is irresistible, charming, seductive, handsome, witty, commanding. ... The degradation doesn't stick to (him) ... it is all absorbed by his female counterpart, the 'slut', Jo Van Fleet. ("Shadow" 136)

This chauvinistic portrayal of woman as seen above, and which Enekwe attempts in his poetry, serves to undermine the integrity of women as rational beings while simultaneously establishing them as extremely selfish and self serving species with killer instincts. Hence like the projection of Jo Van Fleet in the movie, any time we encounter Enekwe's archetypal "women" "we are embarrassed every time she appears on the screen, because every time, she is humiliated further" (136). Such notions of female irrationality and invisibility as offered by Enekwe in his poetry find explication in the Nigerian critic's expose about women of Yoruba whose culture has made it such that:

women are 'naturally' excluded from public affairs; they are viewed as unable to hold positions of responsibility, rule men or even be visible when serious matters of state and society are being discussed. Women are viewed to need tutelage before they can be politically active..." (Ogundipe-Leslie 130)

Further in the poem "Prayer for Peace" Enekwe's recourse to his cherished masculinist theme is done with a touch of irony where men are presented as innocent victims (and acolytes) at the "altar" of feminine abuse. Hence they resort to 'prayer' to deflect the evil of femininity. Once again, the subject matter here, sex, is seen to wield a disastrous outcome on humanity. Employing a Hellenistic metaphor (Troy), Enekwe evokes scenes of destruction and disaster unleashed on "bewildered children crying to heaven" and wretched "widow(s) in black" who join the "funeral train" to the place of burials. The cause for such grand destruction, we are told, lies in the mythical powers of the sexual organ, as symbolized by the "lifted thigh." Here female sexuality is misprised as wreaking only havoc and destructive violence on man. The "thigh" is of quasi religious power and significance and as such becomes an image and instrument of disaster.

> your lifted thigh
> deflects the planets
> disturbs the seas
> floods farmlands. (31)

The woman's ability to destroy man throughout the ages, as the poem suggests, is entrenched in her sexuality which the poet vulgarizes as

> …the corrosive liquid of passion,
> the pulverization of flesh
> in the intensity of copulation. (31)

This supposed power of woman over man can only be calmed with prayers, ubiquitous sacrifices and supplications as suggested in the last stanza of the poem:

> Queen of fire
> be steady and calm
> ...
> open to peace the gates of the city. (32)

Here the poet entrenches the notion of male rational balance by resorting to the myth of an opposing irrational female power. The poet's dilemma here is similar to that posed by Bishop's "The Fish" which Patricia Yaeger rationalizes as dilemma of killing "the object" in order to "assert the subject." As she comments,

> the question in other words, is how one writes poetry about an "other" who has an extra-human power the self thinks it needs, without destroying that other's alienness. Should the poet kill the fish, eat him, absorb him? If she refuses she may relinquish the possibility of internalizing this venerability and relinquish as well the enactment of a ritual moment of empowerment, of making herself greater than she was before by absorbing his tremendum. ("Sublime" 195)

However Enekwe, unlike Bishop, does not have to kill his "Helen" physically in order to internalize her "tremendum." He redirects his quest into quasi religious realms where ultimately the object (woman) is supposedly conquered (calmed) by her worshipping acolytes. Thus, it is still a woeful tale of subjugation and abuse, cleverly crafted in lyrics of admiring denouncements prior to the final conquest. Hence under thorough investigation, such powers as suggested by the poet (all lost in mists of myths) do not actually exist.

The Madonna

This is one other portraiture of woman in Enekwe's poetry using the Madonna image where women are only seen and heard through her power and ability to nurture and protect their children. It is ubiquitously sustained in poetry of Africa of pre-independence and postcolonial periods by Diop and Senghor. The archetypal mother-and-child is readable in the following poems of Enekwe: "To Mother on her birthday" (Broken Pots), "Black woman" (Marching to Kilimanjaro), "That I could Fly" and "Nneka" (Gentle Birds Come to me).

In "To Mother on her Birthday," Enekwe begins his stereotype of woman as nurturing symbol, self sacrificing and long suffering. In the first stanza, the poet seeks to establish the reason for this relationship:

> ... you did more
> than bring us into the world
> and let us suck life
> from your nipples. (11)

Maternal duty is offered as the raison d'etre for the survival of feminine identity. Here she is stable and self-sacrificing. Maternal love is "a love that thrives like Iroko" (Pots 12) in its all embracing nature. Mother's voice is "beautiful as dawn" and "...sweet as songs woven by black birds among sunflowers" (Gentle 38) because she "nurtured and tended" her children. Her tender care gives the suckling baby

> sweet sensations (that) rises in pressure
> Tiny legs kick with pleasure
> Sleep comes gently and strong
> Sleep whispers softly and long. (9)

Her self-sacrificing nature is observed through her understanding that

> ... to love her baby
> is to bathe her and wipe
> her nostrils, mouth and rump. ("Mother" Pot 12)

As Mother she knows it is her duty to caution and sympathize:

> My child, you may rove
> to discover the world
> but do not follow everything
> that pleases your eyes. ("Fly" Gentle 38)

And for the poet, as for Okonkwo's uncle in the classic African novel Things Fall Apart by Chinua Achebe, "Mother is supreme."

Outside of these roles the mothering woman does not have an identity of her own. As Tompkins opines, women are "used as extensions of men, mirrors of men, devices for showing men off, devices for helping men get what they want. They are never there in their own right, or rarely...." ("Shadows" 136). In this instance, as Enekwe suggests in his poems, women get recognized as a result of their role as mothers. Once this dubious stamp is removed or deflated, we may assume that the woman ceases to exist. To Enekwe, the ideal woman is a symbol of nurture (or perhaps self-torture and self-annihilation) which the poet mischievously equates with succor, endurance, self-sacrifice, patience, tolerance, wisdom, hard work and suffering. This steadfast love and stoicism of a suffering woman is likened to Africa which the poet refers to as "Queen of perpetual smile /and gentle, flowing sadness" and one whose "warm breasts/ light the corridors of life" (Kilimanjaro 29)

In line with this image of African womanhood fostered in the tradition of leading Francophone poets like Leopold Senghor, Africa was to endure and forgive its colonial rape and degradation and moreover is expected to continue this endurance with long suffering platitudes such as Enekwe offers. But as Mariama Ba opines, "we no longer accept the nostalgic praise to the African mother who, in his anxiety, man confuses with mother Africa." (qtd. in Schipper 47). Obviously Enekwe's perception of womanhood betrays this element of anxiety foreshadowed by Ba. Thus there is need for cultural sterilization which will overhaul such idealization and romanticisation of African womanhood because as Florence Stratton observes "through the Mother Africa trope, they (men) mask the subordination of women in the patriarchal socio-political systems of African states from which they do, indeed, need to be liberated." (55). There is also need to project women in all entirety as literary subjects with complexities that men are endowed with. As Patricia Waugh opines of this subjectivization,

> once women have experienced themselves as 'subjects' then they can begin to problematize and to deconstruct the socially constructed subject positions available to them, and to recognize that an inversion of the valuation of 'maleness' and 'femaleness' will not in itself undermine the social construction of masculinity and feminity. (25)

Enekwe's projection of these feminine archetypes only succeeds in perpetuating myths that subjugate and undermine womanhood. However as has been attempted by Chinua Achebe and Ngugi wa Thiong'o in their more recent works, there is indeed need for male writers to overhaul the limited portraiture of their women and womanhood so as to reconstruct more positive visioning of womanhood in the literature of modern Africa.

Chapter 10

Women, Race and Liberation

D Sarikaya

FRED D'Aguiar the black British poet whose poetry gives voice to the problems of black immigrants who were considered as the problem groups by the British public during the 1970s and the 1980s was born in England but was sent back to Guyana at age two to live with his grandmother during his childhood (Slade 1). His work showcases the problem of racism and its negative effects on the lives of women and black people. He concentrates on both contemporary racism and colonial racism, and the psychological trauma caused by racism. D'Aguiar inclines to dwell upon the cultural alienation and psychological isolation of the female folk in a completely foreign society, and their feelings of exile in a different society together with their desire to return back to their black African roots. Our aim here, therefore, is to study Fred D'Aguiar's poetry in terms of the problems of immigration and racism which shape social and political circumstances of Britain during the 1970s and the 1980s.

Racism, an "ideology of racial domination based on (i) beliefs that a designated racial group is either biologically or culturally inferior and (ii) the use of such beliefs to rationalize or prescribe the racial group's treatment in the society" (Bulmer and Solomos 4), has been a highly contested issue playing a socially and politically important role on the contemporary global platform. Attributing different origins to each human community, racism aims at creating cultural, social and class barriers between people. The configuration of racial issues in contemporary Britain goes back to the social, economic and cultural impact of mass immigration after World War II, which took place after the loss of the British empire at the end of the 1940s (Solomos 3). The gradual racial re-structuring of Britain has been determined by its economic and Capitalistic interests which were essentially instrumental in regulating immigration to Britain (Brown 7). The homogenised structure of Britain is changed into a multiracial structure; as stated by Ian Spencer, "Britain had ceased to be a white man's country" (2). This multiracial structure brought about a series of problems for the black people like "struggles to achieve equal opportunity, fairness in criminal justice system, equal access to good housing and obtaining satisfactory education" (Goulbourne 75). The problems of "health, social and community services" were the issues that immigrants had to face during the process of their integration into British society (Goulbourne 75). Entangled within such unpredicted problems as an outcome of immigration, Britain found itself endeavouring to restructure its social, political and economic laws according to the problems of immigrants. Black immigration was conceived as a threat endangering the British way of life since those people who immigrated to Britain, instead of incorporating themselves into the mainstream British culture, tried to preserve their own racial identity by creating a kind of counter-cultural identity in opposition to Britishness. According to Teresa Hayter

Immigration controls embody, legitimate and institutionalised racism. They have both been caused by and caused a racism which has become deeply embedded and widely manifest in the rich nation states of the West, and especially so in their apparatus of control, including the police, the immigration authorities and private security guards. Immigration controls have their origins in racism. Time and again, in the history of controls, it becomes clear that the reason for them is not excessive numbers of immigrants, or any realistic assessment of immigrants' effects on jobs, housing, crime or health, but the supposed 'non-assimilability' or 'inferior stock' of certain immigrants. (21)

Thus the resultant social upheavals in opposition to Britain's open door policy of immigration helped in shaping the public mind about the issues of race and immigration. Waters argues that "Contemporary discourses of national decline" caused by the presence of immigrants as "perceived threats to national cohesion" contributed to the creation of stereotypes and negative images of black and coloured people (216). Meanwhile, "focusing on the supposed social problems of having too many black immigrants" social and political debates in Britain were circulated around stopping immigration and preventing the entry of new immigrants who were perceived as a problem (Solomos 52). As a consequence black people on the social and political level began to "resist against discrimination in the form of demonstrations, protests, and 'riots'" while black British poets on the artistic platform became with "cultural forms to register their grievances, express solidarity, and contest the politics of representation" (Childs 194).

Fred D'Aguiar as a black British poet deals with the "question of victimisation" of black people in Britain during the 1970s and the 1980s (Draper 204). D'Aguiar tries to show that the cause of the problem is not black existence in Britain, but the racist hostility of white Britain which is reluctant to embrace its black population and pushes them to the peripheries of mainstream society. In this respect, repudiating the current public opinion about the black population as the "enemy within", D'Aguiar demonstrates clearly in his poetry that it is almost impossible to survive in a society in which there is extreme form of racism, brutality, and hostility towards black people (Gilroy 45).

In the title poem of *Mama Dot* (1985), a book which is based upon D'Aguiar's and his grandmother's experiences of Caribbean village life in Guyana (Forbes 1), D'Aguiar mourns the issue of the double subjugation of slave women. "Mama Dot" is the first poem of the volume, in which the poet summarises the life of his grandmother in a few simple words:

  Born on a sunday
   In the kingdom of Ashante

   Sold on monday

into slavery

Ran away on tuesday
cause she born free

Lost a foot on wednesday
When they catch she

Worked all thursday
till her head grey

Dropped on friday
Where they burned she. (1-12)

The poet uses the days of the week to sum up his grandmother's whole life story which is full of pain and suffering. The use of days to summarise the life of grandmother creates an effect of shortness and simplicity of grandmother's life which is short enough to fit into seven days. From the very beginning of her life, she has to live as a slave and her struggle to get her freedom results in her being exposed to a harsher treatment and mutilation, that is, the loss of her foot. The poet in these lines emphasises the fact that slavery stands as the only inevitable destiny of black people who are born as slaves, and death is the only way to liberation.

While D'Aguiar deals with colonial racism in "Mama Dot", he deals with the contemporary racism in "Black Ink", published in *British Subjects* (1993). "Black Ink" is an important poem which shows the power of the media in alienating the black population in the United Kingdom:

> Reading the Sundays I wash my hands
> Four or five times. I never lick my fingers
> To turn the pages; not since 1982 when I read
> *The Name of the Rose*- the way those monks died.
> (1-4)

D'Aguiar's witty style is felt from the beginning of the poem when the persona takes up a Sunday newspaper to read it. The biased attitude of the media to the problem of racism is underlined through the persona's suspicion that the paper might be poisoned. Making a reference to Umberto Eco's novel *The Name of the Rose*, the persona parallels himself to the monks who were poisoned by licking their fingers while reading Aristotle's *Poetics*. The persona's insecurity leads him to be suspicious of everything, and he thinks that when he licks his fingers to turn the pages, he will be poisoned by the papers. These lines can be read metaphorically to imply the provocative attitude of the media towards racial issues and stirring up of racial hatred. In the following stanzas, the poem focused on the concept of blackness:

> My skin reacts against the detergent in soap
> Forcing me to use a cocoa-butter moisturiser,
> This in turn attracts more newsprint.
> If unwashed, my hands would shine ebony,
>
> No blacker. I note how yesterday my tone
> Was lighter; how today rain insists,
> In a scherzo belted out like an old 78,
> On blackening this city's red brick walls. (9-16)

The persona's hands are blackened by the newsprint so that he needs to wash his hands. Talking about his skin's reaction to the soap which forces him to use a moisturiser, the persona's hands are further blackened by the newsprint. He tries to get rid of this blackness by washing his hands. According to McLeod, "the image of newsprint blackening the speaker's hands literalizes the ways in which the media is complicit in promoting a posionous racializing rhetoric which converts an 'ebony' hand into part of a 'black body', just as the rain insists on 'blackening this city's red brick walls'" (172). As McLeod states, the persona in the poem finds a comparison between his own self and the city whose walls are blackned as the rain falls. Just like the city's brick walls are blackened by the rain, he also feels blackened both literally and metaphorically as he reads the newspapers. He is literally blackened because of the black ink of the newsprints, and he is metaphorically blackened because of the racially intense provocative media which shows the black population as the source of racial problems. The last stanza of the poem comments on the context of the newspapers:

The news is hot, hungry, exclusive after
Exclusive with respected bylines,
Matching action-pictures and written in
Trick ink which disappears as it dries. (17-20)

In this description of the news, the word "exclusive" is especially important because of the fact that just like the news items are excluded from each other by bylines, the news is also characterised as exclusive because black people are separated from the society by the news. Furthermore, the title of the poem is also significant in that the media uses black ink which further blackens the minorities by associating them with criminal activity and promoting stereotypes and racial prejudices against blacks, and thus excluding them (Balkaran 1). In the last line of the poem, the black ink is described as "trick ink" which deludes people by making false news about black people by further blackening and accusing them of being the source of the problems.

Fred D'Aguiar also gives voice to the suffering of a slave in his poem "At the Grave of an Unknown African" published in *British Subjects*. The poem consists of two parts; in the first part the persona is a black British who stands at the grave of an unknown African while in the second part, the persona is the dead African himself. In part I, the persona compares himself to the dead African by comparing the past times of slavery with the present:

> African slave without a name. I'd call this home
> By now. Would you? Your unknown soldier's tomb
>
> Stands for shipload after shipload that docked,
> Unloaded, watered, scrubbed, exercised and restocked
>
> Thousands more souls for sale in Bristol's port;
> Cab drivers speak of it all with yesterday's hurt.
> (11-16)

Although the persona living in England perceives it as his home, he is doubtful about whether the dead African would think England as his home because of the simple fact that he was brought to England as a slave centuries ago during the slave trade. The persona later concentrates on British slave trade and transportation of slaves from Africa to the Bristol port for sale. As James Rawley states, "in the late seventeenth century and during the first three decades of the eighteenth, London dominated the British slave trade. Eclipsed by the West Coast ports of Bristol and Liverpool in midcentury, London recovered over Bristol in the last half-century of the trade" (18). Once the persona thinks about the dead African slave, his mind goes back in time and he begins to think about slavery itself and the lives of those slaves who were transported to Bristol. Later the persona's mind switches to the present, compares the present day experiences of the blacks to the dead African who lies peacefully in his grave:

St Paul's, Toxteth, Brixton, Tiger Bay and Handsworth:
Petrol bombs flower in the middle of roads, a sudden growth

At the feet of police lines longer than any cricket pitch.
African slave, your namelessness is the wick and petrol mix.

Each generation catches the one fever love can't appease;
Nor Molotov coctails, nor when they embrace in peace.
(19-24)

The place names that are mentioned in the poem, St Paul's, Toxteth, Brixton, Tiger Bay and Handsworth are the areas of growing "outbreaks of unrest" in the 20th century where the racial conflicts between the black people and the police force resulted in violence on the both parts (Solomos 143). After describing the hard living conditions in a war like atmosphere among the petrol bombs and Molotov cocktails, he underlines the fact that the namelessness of the African slave and the other slaves like him are the igniters of the fires for black people to resist against the police force. In other words, the persona emphasises that the present generation of black people are taking the revenge of their ancestors who were enslaved and sold as property and who did not even have a name.

While the persona tries to understand the feelings of the dead African slave in the first part of the poem, the dead African slave becomes the persona in the second part of the poem. He begins his speech with a rebuke to the first persona and states:

> Stop there black Englishman before you tell a bigger lie
> You mean me well by what you say but I can't stand idly by
>
> The vandal who keeps coming and does what he calls fucks
> On the cool gravestones, also pillages and wrecks.
>
> If he knew not so much my name but what happened to Africans,
> He'd maybe put in an hour or two collecting his Heinekens.
> (1-6)

He opposes the speaker in the first part who claims that the unknown African who lies in his grave is unaware of what is happening in the present day, and how hard life is within racial conflicts. The persona claims that he is not blind about the things going on around his grave. His grave is destroyed and harmed by the Whites whom he calls vandals. He further states that those people could have the chance to know what happened to Africans in the past, they would have shown a little respect to their grave by collecting their beer-cans. In brief, Fred D'Aguiar, in this poem, tries to show that race and racism still continue to be a major problem in Britain, by making a comparison between the past and present. The black population are still exposed to the same treatment of subordination and discrimination. Although they are not slaves any longer, black people continue to be the targets of racial hatred either by the white population or by police brutality. They are forced to live under the shadow of police control.

The categorisation of the black people as a problem group is also illustrated in detail in another poem by Fred D' Aguiar, "Ballad of the Throwaway People" published in *British Subjects*. D'Aguiar specifically brings to attention the operation of racial discrimination in almost every social institution, and shows the isolation of the black population as a result of racially motivated legislations against immigration. D'Aguiar expresses the feelings of animosity of the black people as follows:

> We are the throwaway
> people
> The problem that won't go away
> people
> ... ...
> The we have no use for you
> people
> The blood we had to have was tainted
> people. (1-4, 9-12)

Black people are explicitly defined as the problem in this poem. The poet reacts with frustration and anger with the hostile living conditions of the black people who, as victims of racism, frequently find themselves in conflict with British society which sees the presence of the black population as a great problem, disrupting the peace and security of contemporary Britain. The physical structure of the poem is also significant. The lines consist of long and short lines which complete each other meaningfully but the repeated words "people" are all separated from the previous lines to imply the marginalisation of black people from the rest of the society. After referring to the discrimination and exclusion which leave the black people in isolation, the poet underlines the dominant hegemonic discourse of the black race being inferior to the white race as it is expressed explicitly in line 11. The poet further continues to delineate how little value is given to the black people whose life seems useless:

>The priests are reluctant to bury
>people
>The buried at the edge of cemeteries
>people
>The keep your grief private
>people
>The world has no love for us
>people. (21-28)

D'Aguiar gives voice to the difficulties of living in a world that has no love for black people. Not only in life, but also after their death black people are given no value. The title of the poem "Ballad of the Throwaway People" is also significant. The Ballad, as a literary form, is part of a song tradition telling a generally tragic story in a simple language, told through dialogue and action (Cuddon 71). The poem, in this respect, is a ballad of "throwaway people", song of black people who are *Othered* by the society. The poem narrates the tragedy of black people who find it difficult to live in a hostile society. The operation of racism at first glance seems to be the social, political and economic segregation of the black people in the inner city areas, but closer examination reveals its deep psychological dimensions on the life of the black people who develop a sense of worthlessness as an outcome of racism. D'Aguiar, in this poem, puts emphasis on the impact of racial exclusion on the life of black people who are separated from their origins, marginalised in the society, discriminated, pushed away and abused in the streets, and refused by British society.

Furthermore, the poet becomes more specific in his criticism of the deteriorating living conditions of black people, and goes further in his exploration of institutional racism in another poem called "Inner City". In this poem, D'Aguiar explicitly demonstrates the tremendous realities of the inner city areas of Britain where the white and the black dichotomy reached its peak. The corruption within the institution of the police force as an instrument of oppression and exploitation is pinpointed; he says:

> Who's to knock their heads together
> Now that the bobby on the beat
> is part of the gang you meet at night
> roaming the city's streets,

>   brazen in their uniform,
>   smiling through clenched teeth? (7-12)

The police force which is patrolling the streets of the inner city areas with the supposed aim of providing security, itself constitutes a threat for the security of people. Living in the inner city areas in poor conditions, the black population that is associated in discourse of racism with criminality and violence have themselves become victims of police violence. The order and neatness of the police officers' clothes are in complete contradiction with the corruption of the police institution. The reason of this corruption apparently is the fact that racism is institutionalized within the state apparatuses which cause social, cultural, economical and political inequalities within the society. As Sivanandan states, racism is an instrument of discrimination and exploitation:

> In Britain, with its long tradition of racism over five centuries and three continents, racial prejudice has become an intrinsic part of popular culture, racial discrimination has come to inhere in the institutions of the society and racist laws and policies have characterised state intervention at the point of economic need….In sum, the laws, the administration, the criminal justice system- the whole state apparatus in Britain- is rife with racism and gives the lie to the government's pretensions to counter institutional racism and the culture which gives it a habitation and a name. (2, 3)

Therefore, racism, which is institutionalised within the criminal justice system and other institutions, leads to the overrepresentation of black people and the inevitable stigmatisation of blacks as criminals in the view of the police as well as the general public. The idea that the blacks are the source of social problem proves itself to be wrong as it is explicitly revealed in this poem. In the following part of the poem, a specific incident of the killing of a black girl is reported:

> The children report the attack
> as something miraculous. One says
> he heard the girl's bones crack.
> Another liked how the dog wagged
> throughout. A third bragged
> that after a while it was hard
> to tell the colour of the ground
> from the girl's smooth brown:
> both were dug-up, both were raw;
> both were under English law.
> The children grow up feeling like dogs,
> they worship stumps for gods. (19-30)

With the aim of reflecting the desperate situation of the inner city areas which are characterised with poverty and crime, the poet brings forth the subordination of people to the intolerable living conditions caused by the failure of law and order in the society. The police, far from solving the problem, constitute the most important part of the problem. Moreover, another striking point that needs to be emphasised is the children that witness the attack on the black girl. Children should be normally expected to be sensitive to the awfulness of the situation but, on the contrary, they report the violent event as an exciting miraculous incident because of the simple fact that violence has become an integral part of everyday life in the inner cities. What is more shocking in the poem is that children almost delight in violence and bloodshed and brag about it as if it were something positive. The "wagging" of dogs is also important which shows that even the dogs feel joy and happiness in this violence. After emphasising the failure of the British law system to improve the poor living conditions of the inner city, the poem ends with a hint of foreboding. Children who are brought up in such living conditions are accustomed to violence and eventually turn out to be criminals by losing their humanity.

Both the "Ballad of Throwaway People" and the "Inner City" show that Fred D'Aguiar specifically draws attention to the problem of racism which makes life difficult for black and coloured people in Britain. D'Aguiar's poetry reflects how racism turns out to be a crucial problem in contemporary Britain, causing the escalation of tensions between the blacks and the whites and creating polarisation in the society.

Fred D'Aguiar's "Letter from Mama Dot" included in *Mama Dot*, is based on the idea of racial identity of those who did not immigrate to Britain and preferred to remain in their homeland. The poem is written from the point of view of a grandmother in the form of a letter to her grandson. The poem consists of two parts and in the first part, the grandmother points out the social and economic deterioration in Guyana:

> Your letters and parcels take longer
> And longer to reach us. The authorities
> Tamper with them (whoever reads this
> And shouldn't, I hope jumby spit
> In them eye). We are more and more
> Like another South American dictatorship,
> And less and less part of the Caribbean.
> Now that we import rice (rice that used to grow wild!)
> We queue for most things:
> Flour, milk, sugar, barley, and fruits
> You can't pick anymore. I join them
> At 5 a.m. for 9 o'clock opening time,
> People are stabbing one another for a place
> And half the queue goes home empty-handed,
> With money that means next to nothing. (1-15)

The grandmother's letter depicts the economic, social and cultural deterioration which have shaped black historical experience not only during slavery but also after slavery. The present situation of Guyana which is founded upon the ruins of colonial exploitation is displayed in the poem. Guyana is drained out of its resources, and its people are trying to survive in extreme wretchedness, poverty and misery. The grandmother's comparison of the previous situation of Guyana where rice along with the other foods grew naturally in the environment and the present day situation of Guyana where they have to import them is significant in its demonstration of the paralysing results of colonialism. It is further emphasised that the authorities, instead of dealing with the social problems like unemployment and poverty, turn out to be dictators trying to exert a strict control over people. The grandmother's observations, like her wishing a "jumby spit in dem eye" (4-5) of those who read and control the letters, in fact, pinpoints a crucial understanding of the political subordination of black people as it is argued by Brian L. Moore:

The third facet of the process of subordinating the Creole section in social and economic terms was by hindering the growth of an economically independent peasant and small farming sector as a viable alternative to the plantation system. The very problems which facilitated the intervention of the central government in village affairs and its eventual exercise of absolute control over village administration formed the basis of economic decay of the villages. (118)

As Moore further argues, the emphasis on the poverty of the villagers shows the impact of colonial exploitation which systematically strives to keep ex-colonial countries under subjugated position. Through a grandmother figure, the poet succeeds in shedding an unbiased light on the social and political circumstances of Guyana. In an interview D'Aguiar says:

I've been interested in history, specifically black history, since my first book of poems, *Mama Dot*, about my grandmother in Guyana who is of African descent. My interest in ancestry beyond those who are alive is really my attempt to fill in the gaps of an eradicated past and to understand history through personality, through people and their experiences rather than by a rehearsal of dates and events. A society is best understood by a study of its treatment of the poor and powerless in it. The seeds for regeneration in society frequently come from the bottom, from the least empowered people as a result of their agitation, hunger and invention, and travels upwards, whereas the decay in that society, a society's decadence, its early signs of death, works its way from the top to the bottom. (Frias 418)

D'Aguiar points out that his grandmother is a historical figure, constructing a bridge between the poet and his past. The grandmother functions like a living memory for the poet who is continuously reminded of the colonial history which sums up the cultural elimination, economic exploitation and political assimilation of the colonised people.

In the second part of the poem, the grandmother's focus shifts from Guyana to Britain, to reflect the hard living conditions of immigrants, and she tries to speculate on the white population's view of the black people who will always remain aliens. Her feelings of despondency are expressed in the following lines:

You are a traveller to them.
A West Indian working in England;
A Friday, Tonto, or Punkawallah;
Sponging off the state. Our languages remain pidgin, like our *dark, third,*
Underdeveloped, world. I mean, their need
To see our children cow-eyed, pot-bellied,
Grouped or alone in photos and naked,
The light darkened between their thighs.
And charity's all they give: the cheque,

> Once in a blue moon (when guilt's
> A private monsoon), posted to a remote
> Part of the planet they can't pronounce.
> They'd like to keep us there.
> Not next door, your house propping-up
> Theirs... (1-15) [italics are original]

The grandmother warns her grandson about the crucial fact that, regardless of his attempts to be incorporated into mainstream British society, he will forever remain an outsider. By referring to the strongly established stereotypes about Afro-Caribbean people who are labelled "dark, third world, underdeveloped, cow-eyed, pot-bellied and naked" (4-5) the grandmother underlines an important issue about the fixity of racial identity of black people who are conceptualised as the other to the Western self. It can be argued that British society tries to preserve the difference between the two cultures by keeping black people at a distance. In this respect, Stuart Hall emphasises the notion of difference which is essential to "giving things meaning by assigning them to different positions within a classificatory system" (236). In the same manner, black people are classified in a position of difference and given meanings through representation. Hall formulates the working of representation and claims:

> Typical of this racialised regime of representation was the practice of reducing the cultures of black people to Nature, or naturalising 'difference'. The logic behind naturalisation is simple. If the differences between black and white people are 'cultural', then they are open to

modification and change. But if they are 'natural'-as the slave-holders believed-then they are beyond history, permanent and fixed. 'Naturalisation' is therefore a representational strategy designed to fix 'difference', and thus secure it forever. It is an attempt to halt the inevitable 'slide' of meaning, to secure discursive or ideological 'closure'. (245)

As Hall argues, the cultural division between black and white is fixed and naturalised through representation. In the poem, the grandmother's allusion to the desire of westerners to see the black Afro-Caribbean people as "cow-eyed, pot-bellied/ Grouped or alone in photos and naked" (7-8), can be considered as part of representation of black people. Black people's difference is naturalised through fixed differences between the British self and the black other. The qualities of being cow-eyed, pot-bellied and naked are indicators of malnutrition, hunger and poverty. In this respect, the representation of blacks as such can be seen as an implication of the desire of the British people to see blacks in a fixed position of poverty and hunger. Moreover, the grandmother in the poem perceives that the reason behind British society's charity shows its desire to keep blacks at a distance. Therefore, through representation, the racial otherness of the blacks is secured; in Hall's words, the racial identity of "the primitive" in contrast with "the civilised world" is firmly established and naturalised via representation (239).

Additionally, Fred D'Aguair's "Colour" published in *British Subjects,* is an important poem displaying the psychological damage of a black man who is afraid of his blackness:

> I woke with the last of my colour on my gums.
> The rest had melted from me and coated the sheets
> Mattress and both pillowcase. I cursed myself
> For sleeping nude as I stood before the mirror.
>
> This pale somebody stared right back and right through me,
> He looked so hard, I had to glance behind myself.
> An involuntary shiver took me over.
> Ghosts after ghost hurdled my grave. I felt the blood
>
> drain from my face. My one thought was, what would I say
> to the cleaner?
> (1-10)

What is emphasised in these lines is the nightmare of a man who discovers that his colour stains the sheets, mattress and pillowcase when he wakes up in the morning in a hotel room. The persona blames and is ashamed of himself, internalising the racist stereotypes about his colour which symbolises "evil, demise, chaos, corruption, and uncleanliness, in contrast to whiteness, which equalled order, wealth, purity, goodness, cleanliness, and the epitome of beauty" (Adam and Moodley 250). Although it is not explicitly expressed by the persona who is just worried about how to explain it to the cleaner, the underlying idea of his nightmare is the revelation of his hidden fears about the colour of his skin which is the primary reason of his sense of inferiority. Fred D'Aguiar comments on the conditions of black communities and points out:

A generation of British-born and bred blacks had come of age only to find that Britishness did not include them. Jobs were not open to them, the police harassed them, there was an increase in racist violence, and subtler forms of racism, such as discrimination in the classroom, meant that black youths were underachieving in school and getting pushed into sport, or else signing on for the dole. This bleak picture fed back into the arts as poets tried to find ways of expressing this experience and articulating creative solutions to it. ("Have You Been Here Long?" 59)

In conclusion, after a detailed analysis of his some of his poems, it can be stated that Fred D'Aguiar's poetry reflects the growing restlessness towards the problem of racism, its becoming social and political concern in Britain and the increasing struggle of the blacks to fight against it. Demonstrating clearly what it is to be black in a British society, D'Aguiar clearly displays the extents of racist violence and exploitation that black people are exposed to (Eldridge 37).

Notes and Bibliography

Chapter 1
Silencing the Abusers

Works Cited

Achebe, Chinua. *Things Fall Apart.* London: Heinemann, 1962.

------. *Anthills of the Savannah.* London: Heinemann, 1988.

Abrahams, Yvette. "Ambiguity Is My Middle Name: A Research Diary." *Women in South African History.* Ed. Nomboniso Gasa. Cape Town: HSRC Press, 2007. 421-452.

Aidoo, Ama Ata. "Unwelcome Pals and Decorative Slaves – or Glimpses of Women as Writers and Characters in Contemporary African Literature." *Medium and Message: Proceedings of the International Conference on African Literature and the English Language* (Calabar, Nigeria: University of Calabar, 1981) 1:17-37.

Andreas, Neshani. *The Purple Violet of Oshaantu.* Oxford: Heinemann, 2001.

Arndt, Susan. *The Dynamics of African Feminism.* Trenton, NJ: Africa World Press, Inc., 2002.

Bâ, Mariama. *So Long A Letter.* Oxford: Heinemann, 1989.

Chiavetta, Eleonora. "A Modern Storyteller." *Sindiwe Magona: The First Decade.* Ed. Siphokazi Koyana. Scottsville: The University of Kwazulu-Natal Press, 2004. 167-173.

Emezue, GMT. "Achebe, Ce." *New Black and African Writing, Vol 1.* Eds. C. Smith and GMT Emezue. Gardena, CA: African Books Network, 2009. 237-260.

Head, Bessie. *The Collector of Treasures.* Oxford: Heinemann, 1977.

Kopf, Martina. "Writing Sexual Violence: Words and Silences in Yvonne Vera's Under the Tongue." *Body, Sexuality, and Gender: Versions and Subversions in African Literatures 1.* Ed. Flora Veit-Wild and dirk Naguschewski. Amsterdam: Rodopi, 2005. 243-253.

Ladner, Joyce A. *Tomorrow's Tomorrow: The Black Woman.* Garden City, NY: Doubleday, 1971.

Lamont, Michèle. *The Cultural Territories of Race: Black and White Boundaries*. Chicago: University of Chicago Press, 1999.

Lorde, Audre. "The Transformation of Silence into Language and Action." *Sister Outsider*. Ed. Audre Lorde. Freedom, CA: The Crossing P, 1984: 40-44.

Magona, Sindiwe. *Beauty's Gift*. Cape Town: Kwela Books, 2008.

Magona, Sindiwe. "Freedom of Expression for Women: Myth or Reality." *Women and Activism: Women's Writer's Conference*. 29-30 July, 1999. Harare: Zimbabwe International Book Fair, 2000. 19-22.

Obbo, Christine. African Women: The Struggle for Economic Independence. London: Zed Press, 1980.

Ogundipe-Leslie, Molara. *Re-creating Ourselves: African Women and Critical Transformation*. Trenton, NJ: Africa World Press, 1994.

Powell, Andrea. "Problematizing Polygyny in the Historical Novels of Chinua Achebe: The Role of the Western Feminist Scholar." *Research in African Literatures*, 39.1 (Spring 2008): 166-185.

Sidikou, Aissata. Recreating Words, Reshaping Worlds. The Verbal Art of Women from Niger, Mali, and Senegal. Trenton, NJ: Africa World Press, 2001.

Solberg, Rolf. "Interview with Sindiwe Magona." *Reflections: Perspectives on Writing in Post Apartheid South Africa*. Eds. Rolf Solberg and Malcolm and Hacksley. Grahamstown: NELM, 1996: 82-99.

Stratton, Florence. Contemporary African Literature and the Politics of Gender. London: Routledge, 1994.

"Stresses and Strains on Black Women." *Ebony*. June, 1974: 33-40.

Vera, Yvonne. *Under the Tongue*. Harare: Baobab Books, 1997.

Weiss, Bettina. "Shades of Utter(ing) Silences in *The Purple Violet of Oshaantu, Maru* and *Under the Tongue*." Journal of African Literature and Culture. 4 (2007):13-32.

Weiss, Bettina. Tangible voice-throwing: Empowering Corporeal Discourses in African Women's Writing of Southern Africa. Frankfurt: Peter Lang, 2004.

Chapter 2
Subjectivity in the 'Eye' of Morrison

Works Cited

Abel, Elizabeth. Race. 'Class and Psychoanalysis? Opening Questions' *Conflicts in Feminism*. Ed. Marianne Hirsch and Evelyn Fox Keller. New York: Rutledge. 1990.

Bertons, Hans. *Literary Theory: The Basics*. New York: Rutledge, 1970.

Bouson, J. Brooks. *Quiet as it's kept: Shame and Trauma and Race in the Novels of Toni Morrison*. Albany: State University of New York, 1999.

Bryson, Valery. *Feminist Debates*. Hong Kong: MacMillan, 1999.

Demetrakopolous, Stephanie. 'Remembering Our Foremothers: Older Black Women, Politics of Age Politics of Survival as Embodies in Novels of Toni Morrison.' *Women and Politics*,1986.

Easthope, Antony. *The Unconscious*. London: Rutledge, 1999.

Feng, Pin-China. The Female Bildungsroman by Toni Morrison and Maxine Hong Kinston.1998.

Grosz, Elizabeth. *Jacques Lacan: A Feminist Introduction*. New York : Norton. 1990.

Lacan, Jacques. *Ecrits: A Selection*. Trans. Alan Sheridan. New York: Norton, 1977.

Lane, Christopher. *The Psychoanalysis of Race*. New York: Columbia UP.1998.

McKay, N. *Critical Essays on Toni Morrison*. Web. 08, 2011. <www.newi.ac.uk/rdover/english/more/modern-a.html>

Mitchell, Juliet. *Psychoanalysis and Feminism*. London: Penguin Books. 1974.

Morris, Pam. *Literature and Feminism*. Cambridge: Blackwell, 1993.

Morrison, Toni. *The Bluest Eye*. New York: Plum, 1970.

Palmer, Pauline. *Contemporary Women's Fiction*. New York: Harvester Wheatshef, 1989.

Peach, Linden. *Toni Morrin*. New York: St. Martin's, 1998.

Portales, Marco. *Toni Morrison's The Bluest Eye: Shirley Temple and Cholly*. The Centennial Review. 1986.

Watkins, Susan. *Twentieth Century Women Novelists: Feminist Theory into Practice*. London: Palgrave. 2001.

Waugh, Patricia. *Feminist Practice and Poststructuralist Theory*. Cambridge: Blackwell. 1987.

Chapter 3
Rotimi's Drama and the Gender Issue

Works Cited

Abrams, M. H. *A Glossary of Literary Terms*. London: Wadsworth. 2005.

Ajayi, Omofolabo. "Gender and Revolutionary Ethos of Class in *Morountodun*." Ed. Awodiya Muyiwa. *Femi Osofisan: Interpretive Essays 1*. Lagos: CBAAC., 1996 (88 -104).

Boal, Augusto. *Theatre of the Oppressed*. London; Pluto Press. 1974.

Dako, Kari. "The Female Role as an Indicator of Social Change in R. E. Obeng's *Eighteenpence*. *LARES: A Journal of Language and Literary Studies*. Vol 14. No 1 (2003). 158-181.

Dasylva, A. O. *Dramatic Literature: A Critical Source Book*. Ibadan: Sam Bookman. (1997).

Davies, Carole Boyce. "Some notes on African Feminism."Eds. Tejumola Olaniyan and Ato Quayson. *African Literature, An Anthology of Criticism and Theory*. Victoria: Blackwell Publishing. 2009. 561-569.

Elegbeleye, O.S. and Adeoti, Gbemisola "Reflections on the Dominant Affective Personality of Ola Rotimi as Exemplified in his Tragic Hero Characterisation." Eds. Lekan Oyeleye and Moji Olateju. *Readings in Language and literature* Ife: Obafemi Awolowo University Press Ltd. (2003). 253-264.

Emecheta, Buchi. "Feminism with small 'f'! Eds. Tejumola Olaniyan and Ato Quayson. *African Literature, An Anthology of Criticism and Theory*. Victoria: Blackwell Publishing. (2009). 551-557.

Johnson, Samuel. *The History of the Yorubas*. Lagos: CMS Bookshops. 1966.

Kern, Anita. "Notes on the Evolution of Women in West African Fiction." Eds. Feuser Willfried and I. N.C. Aniebo. *Essays in Comparative African Literature.* Lagos: CBAAC. (2001). 157-176.

Obafemi, Olu. *Collected Plays of Olu Obafemi(1)* Ilorin: Frobim Press. 1986.

Ogundipe-Leslie, Molara. "Stiwanism: Feminism in African Context." Eds. Tejumola

Olaniyan and Ato Quayson. *African Literature, An Anthology of Criticism and Theory.* Australia: Blackwell Publishing. (2009). 542-550.

Osofisan, Femi. "Literature and the Cannibal Mother." Ed. Femi Osofisan, *Literature and the Pressures of Freedom.* Ibadan: Opon Ifa Readers. (2001). 1-24.

– – –.Tegonni*: An African Antigone.* Lagos: Concept Publications Ltd. 2007.

– – –.*Morountodun and Other Plays.* Lagos: Longman. 1982.

Rotimi, Ola *The Gods Are Not to Blame.* London: Oxford UP. 1971.

– – –. *Kurunmi*: An Historical Tragedy. Ibadan: Oxford UP. 1971.

– – –.*Ovonramwen Nogbaisi*: *An Historical Tragedy.* Benin: Ethiope Publishing Corp. and Ibadan: O.U.P. 1974.

– – –.Our Husband Has Gone Mad Again: An Historical Tragedy in English. Benin: Ethiope Publishing Press Plc. 1974.

Smith, Harold L. Ed. *British Feminism in the Twentieth Century.* London: Edward Edgar Publishing Ltd. 1990.

Sophodes *"Oedipus Rex" The Theban plays.* Harmondsworth Pergium Books Limited. (1975). 22-162.

Soyinka, Wole. *The Beatification of Area Boy.* Ibadan: Spectrum Books Limited. 1995.

Chapter 4
Rethinking the African Woman's Identity

Works Cited

Alkali, Zaynab. *The Stillborn.* Ibadan: Longman, 1984.

Chukwuma, Helen. "Positivism and the Female Crisis: The Novels of Buchi Emecheta" *Nigerian Female Writers*. Ed. Henrietta Otokunefor and Obiageli Nwodo. Lagos: Malthouse, 1989. 2-18.

Davies, Carol Boyce. "Maidens, Mistresses and Maidens: Feminine Images in Selected Soyinka's Works" *Ngambika Studies of Women in African Literature*. Eds. Carole Boyce Davies and Ann Adam Graves. New Jersey: Africa World Press, 1986. 75-88.

Ejinkeonye, Ugochukwu. "Still a Malignant Cancer? Feminism in Nigerian Literature and Society" (2) *Sunday Vanguard*. July 13, 2003: 46.

Emecheta, Buchi. *Second-Class Citizen*. Oxford: Heinemann, 1994.

Encyclopaedia Encarta Premium. Redmond: Microsoft Corporation, 2009. DVD.

Evwierhoma, Mabel. *Female Empowerment and Dramatic Creativity in Nigeria*. Ibadan: Caltop, 2002.

Ezeigbo, Akachi. *Gender Issues in Nigeria: A Feminine Perspective*. Lagos: Vista, 1996.

Killam, Douglas and Rowe, Ruth. *The Companion to African Literatures*. Oxford: James Currey, 2000.

Koenig, Rachael. *Interviews with Contemporary Female Playwrights*. New York: Birch Tree, 1987.

Mohanty, Chandra, Ann Russo and Lourdes Torres (eds). *Third World Women and the Politics of Feminism*. Bloomington: Bloomington Indiana UP, 1991.

Ogundipe-Leslie, Omolara. "The Female Writer and Her Commitment." *African Literature Today*. Vol. 15. Ed. Eldred Jones et al. New Jersey: Africa World Press, 1987.

- - -. *Re-creating Ourselves: African Women and Critical Transformations*. Trenton NJ: Africa World Press, 1994.

Onwueme, Tess. *The Broken Calabash*, Ibadan: Heinemann, 1992.

- - -. *Riot in Heaven*. New York: Africana Legacy, 1996.

- - -. *The Reign of Wazobia*, Ibadan: Heinemann, 1992.

- - -. *Tell it to Women*, Ibadan: Heinemann, 1995.

Oyewùmi Oyèrónke. "Feminism, Sisterhood and other Foreign Relations". *African Women and Feminism: Reflecting On The Politics of Sisterhood*. Ed. Oyewùmi Oyèrónke. Trenton NJ: Africa World, 2003. 1-24.

Sofola, Zulu. "Feminism and African Womanhood." *Sisterhood, Feminisms and Power: From Africa to the Diaspora*. Ed. Obioma Nnaemeka. Trenton NJ: Africa World Press. 1998. 51-64.

Chapter 5
The Conflicts of Fall and Osammor

Works Cited

Adebayo, Aduke. "Tearing the Veil of Invisibility: The Roles of West African Female Writers in Contemporary Times." Feminism & Black Women's Creative Writing Ed. Aduke Adebayo, (Ibadan: AMD Publishers) 1996 (37-56).

Barry, Peter. Beginning Theory. Manchester and New York: Manchester University Press, 2002.

Bungaro, Monica. "Mothering Daughters and the Other Side of the Story in Amma Darko, Ama Ata Aidoo and Nozipo Maraire" African Literature Today 25 (New Directions in African Literature) Ed. E. Emenyonu. New Jersey: Africa World Press, 2006 (76-81).

Cousins, Helen. "Submit or Kill Yourself...Your Two Choices Options for Wives in African Women's Fiction" New Women's Writing in African Literature 24. N.J.: African World Press. 2004 (104-114).

Emecheta, Buchi. The Joys of Motherhood. Ibadan: Heinemann, 2004.

Emenyonu, Ernest. (ed.) Goatskin Bags and Wisdom: Critical Perspective on African Literature. Trenton: Africa World Press, 2000.

Fall, Aminata Sow. The Beggars' Strike. Ibadan: Spectrum, 2002.

Kolawole, M.E.M. "Womanism and African Consciousness". African Literature Today 24 (New Women's writing in African Literature) Ed. E. Emenyonu. New Jersey: Africa World Press Inc., 2004 (104 - 114).

Ogot, Grace. The Promised Land. Nairobi: Heinemann, 1966.

Osammor, Stella Ify. The Triumph of the Water Lily. Ibadan: Kraftgriot, 1996.

Schipper, Mineke. "Buchi Emecheta" Imagining Insiders: Africa and the Question of Belonging London: Cassell, 1999, (189-191).

Chapter 6
The Women of Ousmane and Dlamini

Works Cited

Dlamini, Lucy Z. The Amaryllis. Manzini Swaziland: Macmillan Boleswa Publishers (Pty) Ltd., 2001.

Ousmane, Sembene. Gods Bits of Wood. London: Heinemann Education Books Ltd., 1970.

Bestman, Martin. "Sembene Ousmane : Social Commitment and the Search for an African Identity," in A Celebration of Black and African Writing, eds. King andOgungbesan. Zaria Nigeria: Ahmadu Bello University Press, 1975.

Gates, Henry Louis, Jr., ed. Reading Black, Reading Feminist : A Critical Anthology. New York : Meridian Books, 1990.

Hernton, Calvin C. The Sexual Mountain and Black Women Writers Adventures in Sex, Literature and Real Life. New York: Anchor Press, 1987.

Ikiriko, Ibiwari. "Ousmane's Achievement in God's Bits of Wood" (an M.A. Thesis presented to the Department of English and Literary Studies, University of Calabar, Calabar-Nigeria, April 1983).

Killam, G.D. , ed. "Interview with Ousmane in African Writers on African Writing. London: Heineman Educational Books, 1973. Mnthali, Felix. Yoranivyoto . Glasgow : Dudu Nsomba, 1998.

Mogu, Francis Ibe. Black Male Writing and Black Female Responses in the United States. Calabar Nigeria : Centaur Press, 2002.

- - - A Review of Dlamini's The Amaryllis (Unpublished Mss) Department of English Language and Literature, University of Swaziland, Kwaluseni Swaziland, November, 2003.

- - - Literature and Revolution : A study of Sembene Ousmane's God's Bits of Wood." (unpublished Mss), April, 1990.

Nnaemeka, Obioma, ed. Sisterhood, Feminisms and Power : From Africa to the Diaspora. Trenton, New Jersey : Africa World Press, 1998.

Ogundipe-Leslie, Omolara. "The Female Writer and Her Commitment." Eds. Eldred Durosimi Jones. Eustace Palmer, and Majorie Jones. Women in African Literature Today, vol.15, Trenton, N.J: Africa World Press, 1987.

Ruthven, K.K. Feminist Literary Studies: An Introduction. Cambridge: Cambridge University Press, 1984.

Washington, Mary Helen. "The Darkened Eye Restored: Notes Towards a Literary History of Black Women." Ed. Henry Louis Gates, Jr. Reading Black, Reading Feminist: A Critical Anthology, New York: Meridian, 1990.

Chapter 7
Female Subjectivity in Achebe's Novels

Notes
1 No Longer at Ease is abbreviated to [NLAE]
2 Anthills of the Savannah is abbreviated to [AS]

Works Cited

Achebe, Chinua. No Longer at Ease. London: Heinemann, 1967.

– – – . Anthills of the Savannah. New York: Anchor Press, 1988.

Carroll, David. Chinua Achebe. London: Macmillan, 1980.

Ekpa, Anthonia Akpabio. "Beyond Gender Warfare and Western Ideologies: African Feminism for the 21st Century." Ernest N. Emenyonu. Goatskin Bags and Wisdom: New Critical Perspectives on African Literature. Trenton, NJ: Africa World Press, 2000 (27-38).

Falola, Toyin. Culture and Customs of Nigeria. Westport: Greenwood, 2001.

hooks, bell. "Sisterhood: Political Solidarity between Women." Dangerous Liaisons: Gender, Nation, and Postcolonial Perspectives. Anne McClintock, Aamir Mufti and Ella Shohat. Eds. Minnesota: University of Minnesota Press, 1997. 396-411.

Hyden, Goran. African Politics in Comparative Perspective. Cambridge: Cambridge University Press, 2006.

Khayyoom, S.A. Chinua Achebe: A Study of his Novels. New Delhi: Prestige, 1999.

Mazrui, Ali A. "The Black Woman and the Problem of Gender: An African Perspective." Eds. Mazrui Alamin M. and Willy M. Mutunga. Race,

Gender, and Culture Conflict: Debating the African Condition: Ali Mazrui and his Critics. Vol. 1. Trenton: Africa World Press, 2004 (212-235).

Njoku, Benedict Chiaka. The Four Novels of Chinua Achebe: A Critical Study. New York: Peter Lang, 1984.

Okeke, Philomena E. "Negotiating Social Independence: The Challenges of Career Pursuits for Igbo Women in Postcolonial Nigeria." "Wicked" Women and the Reconfiguration of Gender in Africa. Eds. Dorothy Hodgson L. and Sheryl A. McCurdy. Portsmouth, Heinemann, 2001 (234-251).

Palmer, Eustace. An Introduction to the African Novel: A Critical Study of Twelve Books. New York: Africana, 1972.

Reese, Lyn and Rick Clarke. Two Voices from Nigeria: Nigeria through the Literature of Chinua Achebe and Buchi Emecheta. California, Stanford Program on International and Cross-Cultural Education, 1985.

Chapter 8
Female Sexuality in Bessora's Novel

Works Cited

Bessora. Deux bébés et l'addition. Paris: Serpent à Plumes, 2002.

---. "La question du genre: le cas feminine-masculin," Africultures 35, Jan. 1 (2002).

Bland, Lucy and Laura Doan. Sexology Uncensored: The Documents of Sexual Science. Chicago: University of Chicago Press, 1999.

Butler, Judith. Gender Trouble: Feminism and the Subversion of Identity. London: Routledge, 1999.

---. "Performative Acts and Gender Constitution: An Essay in Phenomenology and Feminist Theory." Theatre Journal, Vol. 40, No. 4 (Dec., 1988): 519-531.

---. Undoing Gender. London: Routledge, 2004.

Connell, R.W. Masculinities. Los Angeles: University of California Press, 1995.

De Meyer, Bernard. "La sage-femme, l'éxilée et l'écrivain ou les bébés hybrides de Bessora," French Studies in Southern Africa, No. 36 (2006): 16-30.

Dean, Carolyn. The Frail Social Body: Pornography, Homosexuality, and Other Fantasies in Interwar France. Berkeley: University of California Press, 2000.

Evans, David T. Sexual Citizenship: The Material Construction of Sexualities. London: Routledge, 1993.

McCaffrey, Edna. The Gay Republic: Sexuality, Citizenship, and Subversion in France. Burlington, VT: Ashgate Publishing Company, 2005.

Nagel, Joane. "Ethnicity and Sexuality," Annual Review of Sociology, vol. 26 (2002): 107-133.

– – –. "Masculinity and Nationalism: Gender and Sexuality in the Making of Nations." Ethnic Racial Studies. Vol. 21, no. 2, pp. 242-69.

Preciado, Beatriz. Manifeste contra-sexuel. Paris: Balland, 2000.

– – –. ÒMultitudes queer: notes pour une politique des anormaux," Multitudes, vol. 12, (2003): 17-25.

Schor, Naomi. "The Crisis of French Universalism," Yale French Studies, No. 100, "France/USA: The Cultural Wars." (2001): 43-64.

Storr, Merl. "Postmodern Bisexuality," Sexualities, vol. 2/3 (1999).

Chapter 9
Enekwe's Feminine Archetypes

Works Cited

Abrams, M.H Glossary of Literary Terms. Orlando: Harcourt Brace Jovanovich, 1993.

Melosh, Barbara. Gender and American History since 1890. London: Routledge, 1993.

Ogundipe-Leslie, Omolara. "African women, culture and another Development." Presence Africaine. 1987, 141:1 123-39.

Rice, Philip and Patricia Waugh eds. Modern Literary Theory: A Reader. London: Arnold,1996

Rubin, Gayle. "The Traffic of Women" Toward an Anthropology of Women. Ed. Rayna Rapp Reiter. New York: Ren, 1975.

Schipper, Mineke. "Mother Africa on a Pedestal: The Male Heritage in African literature and Criticism." African Literature Today, 1987, 15:35-54.

Selden, Raman and Peter Widdowson. A Reader's Guide to Contemporary Literary Theory. Kentucky: The University Press of Kentucky, 1993.

Showalter, Elaine. "Towards a Feminist Poetics." Women Writing About Women. Ed. M. Jacobus, London: Croomhelm 1979.

Stratton, Florence. Contemporary African Literature and the Politics of Gender. London: Routledge, 1994.

Tompkins, Jane. "Me and my Shadow." Gender and Theory: Dialogues on Feminist Criticism. Ed Linda Kauffman.Oxford: Basil Blackwell Inc, 1989.

Yaeger, Patricia. "Toward a Female Sublime." Gender and Theory: Dialogues on Feminist Criticism. Ed. Linda Kauffman.Oxford: Basil Blackwell Inc, 1989.

Chapter 8
Women, Race and Liberation

Works Cited

Adam, Heribert and Kogila Moodley. "Psychological Liberation." Racism. Eds. Martin Bulmer and John Solomos. Oxford: Oxford UP, 1999. 250-259. Print.

Balkaran, Stephen. "Mass Media and Racism." 1999. Web. 27.08.2009. <http://www.yale.edu/ypq/articles/oct99/oct99b.html>.

Brown, Ruth. "Racism and Immigration in Britain." International Socialism Journal 68 (1995) Web. 5.06.2006.
<http://pubs.socialistreviewindex.org.uk/isj68/brown.htm>

Bulmer, Martin and John Solomos. Introduction. Racism: A Reader. By Bulmer and Solomos. Oxford: Oxford UP, 1996. 3-17.

Childs, Peter. The Twentieth Century in Poetry: A Critical Survey. London: Routledge, 1999. Print.

Cuddon, J. A. The Penguin Dictionary of Literary Terms and Literary Theory. London: Penguin. 2000.

Eldridge, Michael. "The Rise and Fall of Black Britain." Transition 74 (1997): 32-43.

Forbes, Peter. "Critical Perspective: The Poetry of Fred D'Aguiar." 2001. Web. 28.06.2008. <http://www.contemporarywriters.com/authors/?p=auth26>.

D'Aguiar, Fred. Mama Dot. London: Bloodaxe, 1985.

---. British Subjects. London: Bloodaxe, 1993.

---. "Have You Been Here Long? : Black Poetry in Britain." New British Poetries: The Scope of the Possible. Eds. Robert Hampson and Peter Barry. Manchester: Manchester UP, 1993. 51-71.

Draper, R.P. An Introduction to Twentieth-Century Poetry in English. New York: St. Martin's, 1999.

Frias, Maria. "Building Bridges Back to the Past." An Interview with Fred D'Aguiar. Callaloo 25.2 (2002): 418-425.

Gilroy, Paul. "One Nation Under a Groove: The Cultural Politics of 'Race' and Racism in Britain." Anatomy of Racism. Ed. David Theo Goldberg. Minneapolis: Minnesota UP, 1990. 263-282.

Goulbourne, Harry. Race Relations in Britain since 1945. London: Macmillan, 1998.

Hall, Stuart. Representation: Cultural Representations and Signifying Practices. Walton Hall: The Open UP, 1997.

Hayter, Teresa. Open Borders: The Case Against Immigration Controls. London: Pluto, 2000.

McLeod, John. Postcolonial London: Rewriting the Metropolis. London: Routledge, 2004.

Moore, Brian L. Race, Power and Social Segmentation in Colonial Society. Montreux: Gordon and Breach, 1987.

Rawley, James A. London, Metropolis of the Slave Trade. Columbia: Missouri UP, 2003.

Sivanandan, A. "Poverty is the New Black" Race and Class 43.2. (2001): 1-5.

Slade, Ted. "Poetry Kit Interviews Fred D'Aguiar." 1999. Web.5.06.2009. <http://www.poetrykit.org/iv/daguiar.htm>.

Solomos, John. Race and Racism in Britain. London: Macmillan, 1989.

Spencer, Ian R. G. British Immigration Policy Since 1939: The Making of Multi-Racial Britain. London: Routledge, 1997.

Waters, Chris. "'Dark Strangers' in Our Midst: Discourses of Race and Nation in Britain, 1947-1963." The Journal of British Studies 36.2 (1997): 207-238.

Oral Traditions

WHILE much has been studied by literary scholars of the oral repertoire and their significance for modern writing, attempts to maintain a uni-dimensional study of oral craft have not yielded the desired coherent and contemporaneous application of orality to literature. Ironically, the study of oral literature as a genre existing on its own terms and structures and formulae has only tended to place the traditions in isolation from contemporary literary developments. Regrettably, oral studies (orature) have waned on the syllabi of many African universities as the written form seems to have eclipsed the oral space.

Our commitment to the study in oral traditions is borne from the awareness that African verbal arts still survive in works of discerning writers, and in the conscious exploration of its tropes, perspectives, philosophy and consciousness, its complementary realism, and ontology, for the delineation of authentic African response to memory, history and all possible confrontations with modern existence such as witnessed in recent analyses of the African novel. These studies use multi-faceted theories of orality which discuss and deconstruct notions of history, truth-claim, identity-making, genealogy (cultural and biological), and gendered ideologies.

Our Critical Approaches

Liberian born professor of African languages and literature, founder of the Society of African Folklore, and Literary Society International, LSi, Charles Smith, is editor of the Critical Writing Series on African Literature with Nigerian Chin Ce, books, reviews, copy editor and creative writer. A fellow of the Literary Society International, Ce is also the author of several works of fiction, poetry and essays on African and Caribbean literature.

Our Mission

African Books Network

AFRICAN Books Network with its cosmopolitan outlook is poised to meet the book needs of African generations in times to come.

Since the year 2000 when we joined the information highway of online solutions in publishing and distribution, our African alliance to global information development excels in spite of challenges in the region. Our select projects have given boost to the renaissance of a whole generation of dynamic literature. In our wake is the harvest of titles that have become important referrals in contemporary literary studies. With print issues followed by eContent and eBook versions, our network has demonstrated its commitment to the vision of a continent bound to a common world heritage. This universal publishing outlook is further evidenced by our participation in African Literature Research projects. For everyone on deck, a hands-on interactive is the deal which continues to translate to more flexibility in line with global trends ensuring that African writers are part of the information revolution of the present times.

As one of Africa's mainstream book publishing and distribution networks, writers may look forward to privileged assistance regarding affiliate international and local publishing and distribution service

"Our select projects at African Books Network have given boost to the renaissance of a whole generation of dynamic literature."

www.ingramcontent.com/pod-product-compliance
Lightning Source LLC
Chambersburg PA
CBHW010832230426
43668CB00019BA/2415